Membership Records
of
Seventh Day Baptists
of
Central New York State
1797-1940s

Ilou M. Sanford

HERITAGE BOOKS
2009

HERITAGE BOOKS
AN IMPRINT OF HERITAGE BOOKS, INC.

Books, CDs, and more—Worldwide

For our listing of thousands of titles see our website
at
www.HeritageBooks.com

Published 2009 by
HERITAGE BOOKS, INC.
Publishing Division
100 Railroad Ave. #104
Westminster, Maryland 21157

Copyright © 1994 Ilou M. Sanford

Other books by the author:

First Alfred Seventh Day Baptist Church Membership Records, Alfred, New York

*Membership Records of Seventh Day Baptist Churches in
Western New York and Northwestern Pennsylvania, 1800-1900*

Newport Seventh Day Baptist Trilogy
Ilou M. Sanford and Don A. Sanford

All rights reserved. No part of this book may be reproduced or transmitted in any form or by any means, electronic or mechanical, including photocopying, recording or by any information storage and retrieval system without written permission from the author, except for the inclusion of brief quotations in a review.

International Standard Book Numbers
Paperbound: 978-0-7884-0015-5
Clothbound: 978-0-7884-8098-0

Membership Records of Seventh Day Baptists
in Central New York State

Table of Contents

The Brookfield Group 1
     1st Brookfield, Leonardsville, West Edmeston

DeRuyter 27

The Scott Area 48
       Scott, Lincklaen, Truxton, Preston
       Norwich, Ithaca, Newport, Otselic

Verona Area 75
       1st Verona, 2nd Verona, Syracuse

Adams Center Area 92
     Adams Center, Houndsfield, Watson
     Richland, Diana, Pinckney

List of Abbreviations

```
ad. . . . admitted
d . . . . died
d/o . . . daughter of
dec . . . deceased
dis . . . dismissed
dp . . . .dropped
ex . . . .excluded
excom . . excomunicated
fr . . . .from
gc/o . . .grandchild of
gd/o . . .granddaughter of
gs/o . . .grandson of
nr . . . .non-resident
pos. . . .possibly
prob . . .probably
rem . . . removed
rj . . . .rejected
s/o . . . son of
w/o . . . wife of
wid/o . . widow of
```

Foreword

This is a compilation of hundreds of names and statistics for Central New York state beginning in 1797 when Seventh Day Baptists were often among the first settlers in the area. Original records located at the Janesville Archives were used when they could be diciphered. If records were illegible, lists copied at a later date from earlier records were used. Some secondary records were used to fill in the gaps in an outline of churches in existence in the 1800's time slot. For some churches few records could be found.

Due to the fact that church clerks varied a great deal in what they thought important, there is a wide variety of information: admissions, births, baptisms, deaths, dismissals, excomunications, places of origin, parents, spouses, and biographical tidbits. Infant baptisms were not done.

In order to maintain the flavor of the times, spelling was not corrected. Alphabazing was not done because relationships often show up better as they are written on a page. Editorial comments were used if items were questionable.

IMS:1993

Historical Society time and personnel limits the staff time in personal research of the records. Professional genealogists with access to the files may be individually contracted. The Historical Research Library and Archives are open to the public for personal research upon appointment.

THE BROOKFIELD GROUP
Madison and Otsego Co.'s

First Brookfield 1797- also called Leonardsville, Madison Co.
Second Brookfield 1823-c1987 Madison Co.
Third Brookfield 1823-1942 also called West Edmeston, Otsego Co.
(In 1990 First and Second Brookfield merged.)

FIRST BROOKFIELD
Leonardsville

MANUAL OF THE FIRST SEVENTH DAY BAPTIST CHURCH of BROOKFIELD, NY
1883
The Committee in Behalf of the Church
Brookfield, NY:
H.L. Spooner & Son, Printer 1883
MS 19x.9 B file: Brookfield   p.13-27

Constituent Members Oct. 3, 1797

Eld. Henry Clarke	Elisha Burdick
Dea. William Davis	John Davis
Luke Saunders	Weden Witter
Joshua Maxson	Anna Davis
James Crandall	Elizabeth Burdick
Benjamin Davis	Judith Maxson
Samuel Greenman	Hannah Maxson w/o Paul
Clark Maxson	Hannah Maxson
James Wamsly	Nancy Maxson
	Caty Clarke

Other Members

Nathan Greenman	Susanna Crandall
William G. Greenman	Dorcas Saunders
Nathan Stillman	Phebe Whitford
Ethan Clarke	Sarah Clarke
Joseph Clarke	Thankful Maxson
Nathan Clarke	Anna Maxson
Jared Clarke	Rhoda Coon
Perry Maxson, Jr.	Susanna Clarke
Amos Saterly	Susanna Crumb
Joshua Coon	Hannah Clarke
Saunders Langworthy	Lydia Davis
Benjamin Wigden	Susanna Maxson
Jonathan Potter	Phebe Clarke
Sylvanus Greenman	Hannah Stillman
Joshua Wells	Sabrina Greenman
William Bliss Wells	Lydia Burdick
Dea. Phineas Burdick	Eunice Dye
Peter Wells	Thankful Crandall
Stephen Clarke, Jr.	Martha Potter
Joshua Davis	Polly Burdick
William Franklin	Eunice Satterly
Sylvester Crumb, Jr.	Elizabeth Crandall
Benjamin Colgrove	Prudence Stillman
Reynolds Greenman	Mary Wigden

Samuel Clarke
Hazard Clarke
Joseph Clarke
William Bassett, Jr.
Samuel P. Burdick
Edward C. Clarke
Beriah Babcock
Augustus Crandall, Jr.
William Reynolds
Abraham Lewis
Saunders Crandall
William Bassett
Samuel Babcock, Jr.
Jonah Taylor
Daniel Babcock, Jr.
Charles Burdick
Samuel Babcock
Richard Clarke
Augustus Saunders
Charles Babcock
James C. Burdick
Eli Colegrove
Elisha C. Green
Elnation Wells
Dea. William Utter
Dea. Alfred Maxson
Reuben Bisby
Augustus Saunders, Jr.
Edmund Cotes
Elnation Davis
Lott Crandall
Welcome A. Clarke
Ethan Clarke
Joshua Maxson, Jr.
John Maxson
Benjamin Nye
William Vitter
Abel Burdick
Willet Stillman
Abram C. Crandall
Amos Maxson
Edward Babcock
Paul Crandall, Jr.
Augustus Kenyon
Oliver P. Clarke
Eld. Eli S. Bailey
Silas Spencer

Sylvia Wells
Eunice Randall
Sylvia Kenyon
Maribah Whitford   (Burdick)
Mercy Davis
Sarah Franklin
Ruth Crumb
Persis Maryott
Tacy Maxson (Clarke)
Sally Maxson (Crandall)
Eunice Whitford
Sarah Colegrove
Sarah Greenman
Elizabeth Maryott
Judith Clarke
Nancy Clarhe (Davis)
Hannah Clarke
Phebe Burdick
Lydia Reynolds
Fanny Bassett
Mary Burdick
Elizabeth Lewis
Charlotte Crandall
Nancy Maxson
Thankful Crandall
Nancy Clarke
Rebecca Burdick
Ruth Burdick
Patty Clarke
Betsey Crumb
Peggy Cole
Hannah Burdick
Dorcas Saunders
Judith Colegrove
Syllvia Wells (Bentley)
Nancy Davis (Tift)
Martha Burdick
Martha Crandall
Martha Maxson
Friegiffe Nye
Abigail Nye
Lydia Davis
Serenah Stillman
Sally Potter
Mary Burdick
Hannah Wilcox
Lydia Bisbee
Content Davis
Elizabeth Weaver (Miner)
Lucy Huntington
Polly Babcock
Lois Potter (Babcock)
Mercy Langworthy
Ruth Johnson

		Betsey Clarke
	1809	
Stephen Tanner		
	1810	
		Persie Langworthy
		Lucy Langworthy
	1811	
		Joanna Kenyon
		Susanna Hall
		Elizabeth E. Wells
	1812	
Theodatus Johnson		
	1813	
Felix Millard		Giffy Millard
	1814	
Jonathan Babcock		Polly Kenyon
Paul Clarke		Sally Perkins
		Chloe Clarke
		Tacy Babcock
		Prudence Colegrove
		Patience Colegrove
		Sophia Witter
		Susanna Crandall
	1815	
Ezra Coon		Clary Coon
Samuel Whitford		Betsey Coon
Samuel Cole		Hannah Cole
Hazard Sheldon		Rachel Maxson
Henry Clarke, Jr.		Laura Coon
Amos Burdick, Jr.		Lucy Clarke
Amos Burdick		Caty Burdick
		Lydia Champlin
		Caty Clarke
	1816	
Charles Burdick		Sarah Burdick
Stephen Rose Burdick		Lydia Clarke
Isaac Clarke		Ellen Saunders
David Clarke		Jane White
Harry White		Judith Clarke 2d
Hezekiah Saunders		Thankful Kenyon
Benjamin Burdick		Lydia Champlin
Adin Burdick		Desire Burdick
Nathan Stillman, Jr.		Almira Taylor
Stanton Crandall		Maria Burdick
Nathan Mariot		Avis Burdick
Sylvester Greenman		Esther Utter
Sylvester Maxson		
Peleg H. Bassett		
Amasa Jones		
Ephraim Maxson		
	1817	
Joel Kenyon		Lois Clarke

Godfrey White   Lucy Holton
Gideon White   Deborah Clarke (Maxson)
Henry Crandall   Jane White
Luke Saunders   Susan White
Elliot Smith   Rebecca Saunders
                                                Patty Crandall

                          1819

Eld. Daniel Coon   Almira Greenman
Abel Stillman   Evalina Clarke
Dea. Ethan Stillman   Elsy Simonds
Elias Burdick   Content Stillman
                                                Eunice Saunders

                          1820

John B. Stillman   Dolly Utter
Stephen Whitford   Demis Babcock
Henry Clarke, 3rd M.D.   Tacy Babcock
John Babcock   Ann Lewis
Lewis Bassett   Catherine Dwight
Paul C. Maxson   Lucy Maxson
Clark Stillman   Catherine Sisson
Asher M. Babcock   Dorcas Bassett
Ethan Coon   Phebe Clarke
Jared Covey   Betsy Burdick
Elihu Cleveland   Hannah Williams
John Utter   Susan Clarke
Clark Lewis   Prudence Utter
                                                Patty Babcock (Billings)
                                                Polly Covey
                                                Lucretia Cleveland
                                                Tacy Lewis
                                                Ruah Lewis

                          1821

Jonathan Davis   Polly Maxson (Simons)
Jonathan Davis, Jr.   Susan Taylor (Wilcox)
Paul Witter   Harriet Taylor (Burton)
Phineas Clarke   Mahala Green
Isaac Brown   Rebecca Brown
John V. Clarke   Hannah Clarke
Peleg Babcock   Susanna Lanphere
John Witter   Hannah Taylor
William Bliss Saunders   Rhoda Mills
Samuel Saunders   Patience Witter
Elisha Stillman   Demaris Burch
Nathan Burch   Caty Popple
Samuel L. Babcock   Ruba Witter
Welcome Babcock   Martha Kellogg
Henry Babcock   Sylvia Saunders
Andrew Babcock   Lydia Saunders
Joel Maxson   Miranda Colegrove
Geo. W. Maxson, M.D.   Amanda Clarke
Kenyon Crandall   Ordery Spencer
Samuel H. Coon   Emma Langworthy
Aldrich Crandall   Olive Coon
Ethan Crandall   Nancy Babcock

Ethan Stillman	Phebe Babcock
David Maxson	Mary Crandall
Thomas Williams	Fanny Hall
Darius Chapin, M.D.	Lovinia Maxson
William Simons	Mary Crandall w/o Kenyon
John Davis, 2nd, Esq.	Olive Coon
Lyman Saunders	Mary Crandall w/o Aldrich
William Cole	Electra Crandall w/o Ethan
Daniel Brown	Nancy Clarke
Thomas Dye	Mercy Popple
James Perkins	Betsey Saunders
Ira Spencer	Lucy Ann Davis (Fitch)
Isaiah Robertson	Irena Coon
Joseph Langworthy	Elizabeth Burdick
Elias L. Langworthy	Amy Saunders
Christopher Langworthy	Fanny Stillman
Robert L. Davis	Prudence Clarke
Luke Clark	Hannah Clarke, 2nd
Rogers Davis	Deborah Wilbur
Rowland Coon	Polly Robertson
Jacob Martin	Rhoda Spencer
Isaac W. Brown	Mary Spencer
Solomon Barnes	Fanny Davis (Rogers)
David Burdick	Phoebe Kenny
	Lovina Spencer
	Rosanna Witter
	Nancy Langworthy
	Amy Spencer
	Maria Spencer
	Calista Langworthy
	Betsey Saunders
	Roena Witter
	Marita Witter
	Susanna Langworthy
	Saloma Saxton
	Annathrasia Saxton
	Polly Mills
	Lydia Clarke
	Fanny Wilbur
	Eliza Burdick
	Lucy Ann Langworthy
	Betsey Crumb
	Polly Burdick
	Polly Crandall
	Betsey Wilbur
	Luthy Coon
	Belinda Wells
	Raycab Clarke
	Rachel Maxson
	Lois Davis
	Martha Langworthy
	Recelena Witter
	Clarinda Witter (Wilcox)
	Phoebe Dye (Crandall)

Cynthia M. Clarke
Mahitabel Stillman
Esther Whitford
Esther Crandall

1822

Reuben Wilcox
Eld. William B. Maxson
Nathan Clarke, Jr.
Dea. William Whitford
Elnathan Maxson
John Tanner
Esdras Clarke
Burdick, son Amos
Elnathan Davis
John Utter, Jr.
Calvin Clarke
Nathan R. Brown
William Bassett 3rd
Benjamin Bassett
Cyrus Clarke
Cornwall St. John
Edward G. Lee
Albert Clarke
Hiram Maxson
Archibald K. Crumb
Orran W. Davis
Benjamin Coats

Dorcas Witter
Mary Stillman
Lucy Davis
Lucy Griswold
Esther Covey
Fanny Maxson
Cornelia Maxson
Laura Tanner
Anna Stollman
Aurelia Burdick (Coon)
Hannah King
Grace Coon (Bassett)
Lodemia Clarke
Cordelia Clarke
Lucinda Maxson
Nancy St. John
Sophia Maxson
Eliza Babcock
Mary Stillman
Lucy Bassett
Harriet Bassett
Cornelia Clarke
Lois Greenman
Mary Clarke
Catherine Clarke
Patty Clarke
Catharine Whitford
Betsey Burdick
Lucy Greene
Hannah Greene 3rd
Julia Ann Crumb
Fanny Stillman (Wilcox)
Mary Clarke
Patty Burdick
Esther Palmiter
Mary Clarke
Malvina Greenman
Damaris Crandall

1823

William B. Greenman
Jesse Covey
Dea. Jonathan Burdick
James Crandall, Jr.
Nathan Langworthy
Daniel Burdick
Benjamin Kenyon
Hosea Whitford

Fanny Perkins
Orisa Villa Clarke
Mary Perkins
Harriet Burdick
Celena Covey
Phebe Tift
Orpha Greenman
Variety Green (Stillman)
Achsah Babcock

1824

John Davis, Jr.	Clarissa Tanner
Davis Loofborough	Mary Clarke
Phineas Burdick	Sophia A. Clarke
Stanton Clarke	Eliza Clarke
Thomas Clarke	Electra Hills
Charles W. Dowse	
Willet Stillman, Jr. M.D.	

1825

Ethan Burdick — Betsey Lewis

1826

Peleg Clarke	Rachel West
Clement C. West	Eunice West
Benjamin West	Susan West
John West	Mary Ayars
Ephraim Ayars	

1828

Francis Wilcox	Sophia Wilcox
Israel L. Greenman	Beulah West
Elisha Clarke	Hannah Peck
Roswell Clarke	Patty White
Amos Davis	Mary A. Congdon
Alexander Covey	Clarinda Clarke
Stephen Sisson	Sally Clarke
Asa L. Maxson	Celia Langworthy
Enos Lewis	Eliza Langworthy
Rouse Clarke	Nancy Greenman
William House	Sophronia Ann Davis
Horace Witter	Lydia Millard
Hiland Davis	Fanny Colegrove
Ephraim R. West	Betsey Sweet
Hosea Brown	Ruby Witter, Jr.
Wittis W. Witter	Eliza Clarke
Russel W. Kenyon	Mary Ann Clarke
Nathan L. Bassett	Maria West
Samuel C. Bassett	Saloma Saxton Jr.
Jacob West, Jr.	Hannah Brown
	Polly Lewis
	Sophia Burdick
	Angeline White (Welch)
	Amy Crandall
	Maranda Moor
	Mary E. Clarke
	Sally Burdick
	Diana Seamans
	Maria Crandall
	Clarisa Ann West
	Susan Ann West
	Julia Maxson
	Vid. Nancy Spaulding
	Beulah West
	Orthalinda Langworthy

1829

Eld. Charles Card
John Bowen
Thomas West
Benjamin K. Platts

Olive Card
Mary Ann Sisson
Jane M. Platts
Tacy Saunders (Stillman)
Esther W. Crandall
Dorcas Smith
Fanny Hill
Sibil Millard
Lucy Ann Langworthy

1830

Thomas B. Stillman
Alfred Stillman
Charles Mason
Alvit Clarke

1831

John Cottrel
Nathan M. Burdick
Ransom L. Burdick
Clark Lewis 2nd
Jesse Moon
Truman B. Maxson
Henry Brown
Dea. Jonathan V. Greenman
Joseph T. Crumb
Ebenezer Bass
Paul Stillman
Charles H. Stillman
Jacob B. Stillman
Dea. Geo. B. Clarke
Nelson Clarke
Reuben O. Clarke
Giles Lamphere
Matthew Stillman
Samuel Clarke
Hinkley Greenman
Elisha Babcock
Edwin Maxson
Eld. Charles M. Lewis
Samuel Witter
Rensalaer Nye
Joseph A. Nye
James Cleveland
George T. Davis
Joseph Bassett
Russel E. Crumb
Alonzo Maxson
Henry G. Greenman
Noyes Palmiter

Esther Burdick
Lydia Lanphere
Harriet M. Crumb
Lucy Ann Maxson
Sarah A. Burdick
Esther Lamphere
Hannah Cleveland
Phoebe Clarke (Lewis)
Eliza Ann Babcock
Clarinda Green (Brand)
Harriet Maxson
Phebe Saxton
Lorinda Coon (Clarke)
Alzina Maxson
Harriet Stillman
Nancy Clarke
Martha Millard (Coon)
Prudence Cleveland
Susan Stillman
Adaline Greenough
Margaret Bradt
Melissa Ward (Kenyon)
Eliza Stillman
Maria Stillman (Utter)
Susanna Stillman
Julia Ann Palmiter
Sarah Mattison (Saxton)
Edith Davis
Sally Ann Maxson
Mariam Babcock
Lydia Babcock
Maria Crandall
Nancy Clarke
Susan Bassett
Mary Champlin
Cynthia Witter
Eliza Scott

Mary B. Greenman
Catherine Davis
Alzina Maxson (Walters)
Mercy Baker

1832

Simon Baker
Green Palmiter
Reuben Utter
Ransom Lewis
Clark Saunders
Erastus P. Clarke

Hulda Popple (Burdick)
Catherine Maxson
Julia Ann Clarke
Lois Coon
Amanda Babcock
Keturah Ann Champlin
Elizabeth Greene
Elizabeth Greene (Covey)

1833

Eld. John Greene
Waitstill Phillips

1834

Shefffield W. Greene
Sidney Champlin
John Champlin
Thomas Champlin

1835

David Whitford
Nathan Stillman
Joshua C. Sisson
Joshua G. Sisson
Luther S. Sisson
Clark M. Whitford
Arnold Moon
Maxson Clarke
Welcome Stillman
Truman Saunders
Albert Utter

Fanny A. Sisson (Crandall)
Angeline Clarke (Maxson)
Aurelia Lee (Van Valen)
M. Marie Lanphere
Betsey Whitford
Elizabeth A. Davis
Lucy A. Green (Carr)
Melissa Spaulding
Susan Walker (Simons)
Sarah Greenman
Cynthia Mason

1836

Eld. Henry B. Lewis
Phinny Robinson, M.D.
Ichabod Babcock
Barber B. Stillman
William Woodward
Jabesh Brown, Jr.
William Lawton
Albert Stillman
Eld. Geo. B. Utter

Tacy L. Greene
Sally Maria Clarke
Abby A. Greene
Ann Utter
Sabrina Babcock
Calista Babcock
Phebe R. West
Ruth Crawford

1837

Hazel M. Ayars

1838

Simeon Clarke
Denison Gorton
Joseph Button
Joseph Clarke
Joseph S. Crumb
Eld. Sebius M. Burdick
William Green
Nathan Burch, Jr.

Temperance Burch
Harriet Sisson (Pratt)
Harriet E. Crumb
Mary Baker (Miner)
Sally Maxson (Bassett)
Betsey Ann Mason
Sarah Whitford
Hannah Clarke

Oliver Wilcox   Jane Rogers (Ellison)
John R. Maxson   Naomi Potter
Adison S. Burdick   Betsy Clarke
                                                 Esther Clarke
                                                 Sarah Reynolds
                                                 Henrietta Stillman
                                                 Cornelia Burdick
                         1839
                                                 Amy Crumb
                                                 Cynthia Clarke
                                                 Jane Wilcox (Tracy)
                         1840
John S. Ayars   T. Elizabeth Clark (Green)
                                                 Amanda G. Maxson
                         1842
Ira Millard   Elizabeth Whitmore
Joel G. Saunders   Nancy Burdick
Jonathan C. Burdick   Louisa Clarke
                         1843
Lucien Covey   Amelia Clarke (Blackman)
Grove D. Clarke   Harriet M.W. Stillman
Eld. William C. Whitford   Avis Bassett
Albert Whitford   Lucy Button
Geo. F. Alberti Maxson
Michael M. Saunders
Welcome Miner
George R. Babcock
Francis F. Denison
Samuel Crandall
William Silk
                         1845
Elisha S. Burdick   Jane Burdick
Isaac P. Miner   Esther Crandall
Hiram S. Crandall   Almira Crandall (Clarke)
Loren Wilcox   Catherine Clarke
                         1846
Anson Burdick   Elnora Babcock
Dea. Martin Wilcox   Fanny Wilcox
Sewel S. Maxson   Mahitabel Wilcox
                                                 Sarah P. Wilcox (Potter)
                                                 Josephine Wilcox
                                                 Amanda Burdick
                                                 Elizabeth Lewis (Clarke)
                                                 Widow Betsey Burdick
                                                 Ruth Sattuck
                         1850
Henry Crandall   Octive F. Clarke (Smith)
Wyatt Clarke   Farosina Wilcox
Paul B. Clarke   Lucinda Maxson
Daniel Coon   Mary L. Weaver (Clarke)
                                                 H. Emma Davis
                                                 Sally Crandall
                                                 Polly Edwards
                                                 Betsey Holt

		Elizabeth Saunders
		Lois Burch
		Fanny Maxson
		Catharine E. Edwards
		Elizabeth Millard
	1852	
Benjamin Edwards		Rebecca K. Platts
Samuel N. Stillman		Harriet E. Brown
William Lawton		Julia Ann Crumb
Wm. B.F. Lawton		
	1853	
		Almira E. Burdick
		Marie A. Clarke
		S. Adelaide Corbet
	1857	
Dea. Ransom T. Stillman		Eliza A. Lewis
David Babcock		Eunice A. Stillman
O.D. Sherman		Celestia Clarke
	1858	
Jared Clarke		Ellen A. Robinson
Eld. Oscar U. Whitford		Polly Crandall
Herbert D. Whitford		Maria D. Utter
John L. Clarke		H. Adaline Whitford
LeRoy A. Clarke		Cartha J.V. Clarke
J. Henry Clarke		Lucy B. Angel
Norman L. Burdick		Eleanor G. Porter
Gilbert C. Saunders		Mary Evaline Harder
C. Albertus Saunders		Sarah Whitford
Orlando Angel		Rachel A. Hibbard
F. Hawley Clarke		Rebecca A. Crumb
Edward N. Crandall		Phebe L. Bassett
Milton V. St. John		Eleanor Weaver (Dexter)
Henry E. Bass		Margaret A. Crandall
George Stewart		Lucina Crandall
Andrew J. Robinson		Arloena Clarke
Norris Tarbell		Vernette Moore
Joshua Ayres		
Edgar B. Clarke		
Albert Maxson		
Alanson C. Babcock		
A. Adelbert Washburn		
Henry V. Crandall		
Eli Walters		
DeForest Clarke		
Perry M. Simons		
William Crandall		
Francis R. Covey		
William M. Simons		
	1859	
William M. Robinson		
	1862	
		Mary D. Crandall (Dunn)
		Sibil Whitmore
		Sarah Crandall

1864

Eld. James Summerbell
Squire J. Swann
Dea. Paul B. Burch

Matilda St. John
Hattie Bassett
Celia G. Brand
Rachel Summerbell
Emeline P. Burdick
Emeline Moon
Amy Dennison
Catharine Burdick
Cynthia Burch
Mary Burch (Baylis)

1865

Sarah L. Summerbell
Kate L. Sisson
Mary E. Sisson (Denison)

1866

George H. Angel
Edgar D. Crumb
Nathan F. Clarke
George R. Clarke
Lucius A. Crandall
Louis H. Crandall
Arthur A. Maxson
George W. St. John
Herbert Coon
Frank N. Summerbell
Irving E. Burdick
Albertus Lanphere
Thomas Dye
Charles H. Burdick
William Clarke
Jonathan Hibbard
Sydney T. Langworthy
Samuel D. Whitford
William H. Whitmore

Jane Angel
Lydia A. Browne
Jenette Coon
Mary Eliza Moore
Almira Jane Brand
Lydia Ann Glines
Olive E. Burdick
Alice L. Hall
Orphia E. Davis
Harriet Bassett (Mayne)
Mary F. Summerbell

1868

Eld. Lester C. Rogers

Susan H. Goodrich

1869

Thomas T. Burdick

Harriet V. Burdick
Mary Ann Dowse
Amarintha V. Holmes
Amelia C. Langworthy
Seraphine P. Clarke

1871

Francis J. Clarke
H. Benson Clarke
H. Cliff Brown

Kate E. Burch
Nettie Spencer
Julia Ann Murphy

1873

Celia L. Dowse

1875

William H. Worden

Ella May Green

1876

                                        Eliza Clarke
                            1877
William H. Utter   Caroline E. Brown
Johnnie Brownell
                            1878
                                        Lois Clarke
                            1882
John Green

PRESENT MEMBERSHIP
January 1, 1883

NAMES	RESIDENCE		ADMITTED, DECEASED, DISMISSED
Sally Clarke	Milton, WI		Sep 28, 1816
Sophia Whitford	Leonardsville, NY		Oct 20, 1820
Lucetta Vitter	"		Dec 23, 1820
Betsey Bass	"		Jan 6, 1821
Lucinda Rogers	Brookfield, NY		Jan 29, 1821
Orilla Clarke	Emporia, KS		Apr 30, 1831
Eliza Hardin	Leonardsville		Dec 21, 1822
Jeffrey Champlin	West Edmeston, NY		" " "
Mariam Williamson	Leonardsville		Dec 28, 1822
Salima G. Brown	"	d.	Jan 1823
Anna J. Stillman	"		Nov 1826
Clark Whitford	"		Feb 9, 1828
Asa M. West	"		Apr 26, 1828
Louisa Spaulding	Milton Jct, WI	dis	Jun 28, 1928
Phebe Brown	Leonardsville		Mar 14, 1829
Marilla B. Phillips	Cuba, ILL		" " "
Niles Davis	Milton, WI		Feb 24, 1831
Amos B. Spaulding	Milton Jct, WI	dis	" " "
Lucy B. Hardin	Saginaw City, MI		Sep 25, "
Helen E. Weaver	Leonardsville	d.	" " "
Roswell P. Dowse	"		Oct 8 "
Samuel Clarke	Brookfield		Oct 15 "
Wm Riley Crandall	Eaton		Nov 5, 1831
Harriet Whitford	Leonardsville		Nov 26, "
Ann Royal	"		Sep 29, 1832
Silas Whitford	Brookfield		Sep 27, 1834
Amanda Clarke	Leonardsville	d.	Sep 27, 1834
Louisa M. Davis	Fond du Lac, WI		Dec 25, 1835
Hannah Crandall	DeRuyter, NY		Dec 26, "
S. Emeline Utter	Bridgewater		" " "
Sarah A. Brand	Leonardsville		Mar 9, 1836
Edwin Whitford	"		Mar 31, 1838
Ebenezer S. Weaver	"	d.	Oct, 1840
Lydia L. Langworthy	"		Jun 2, 1838
Hamilton J. Whitford	"		Mar 25, 1843
Eunice Tarbell	Emporia, KS		" " "
Caroline M. Crumb	Belvidere, IL		" " "
Fernando C. Davis	Oysterville, Wash. Ter.		May 28, 1843
Lucina Clarke	Leonardsville		Oct 19, 1845
Juliette Davis	Milton		Oct 25 "
Nelson Clarke	New London		1847
William A. Babcock	Leonardsville		"
J. Delos Rogers	Brookfield		"
Polly Simons	Bridgewater		"
Lucinda Brown	Leonardsville		Mar 30, 1850
Lucinda M. Dowse	"		" " "
L. Eleanor Spicer	Emporia, KS		" " "
Julia A. Rainy	DeRuyter		May 25, "
Sophronia Crumb	Leonardsville		Sep 26, 1851

Name	Location	Date
Harriet Babcock	Leonardsville	Sep 26, 1851
Artemisia O. Maxson	"	Feb 20, 1852
Sarah E. Davis		Mar 26, 1852
Elizabeth F. Brown	"	Mar 25, 1853
Delos C. Whitford	Wocott	Sep 26, 1857
Codelia A. Coon	Leonardsville	Oct 27, 1857
Lucy Ann Clarke	"	Nov 14, 1857
Francis M. Clarke	"	Dec 19, 1857
Adaline A. Sisson	"	Dec 26, 1857
Daniel W. Lee	"	Jan 2, 1858
Susan J. Crandall	"	" " "
Amos L. Clarke	"	Jan 16, 1858
Emily Clarke	Unadilla Forks	" " "
S. Riley Clarke	Leonardsville	Feb 6, 1858
Wm. J. Bass	"	Feb 6, 1858
John T. Rogers	Richburg	Feb 6, 1858
Lydia R. Rogers	"	Feb 6, 1858
Farosina M. Allis	Plainfield, NJ	Feb 6, 1858
Emma O. Crumb	Walworth, WI	Feb 6, 1858
Fidelia Crumb	"	Feb 13, 1858
Mary St. John	Leonardsville	Feb 20, 1858
A. Elizabeth Kinney	Saginaw City, MI	Feb 20, 1858
Reuben D. Ayres	Unidilla Forks	Mar 13, 1858
Juliette Brown	West Edmeston	Mar 13, 1858
Phoebe E. Phillips	Leonardsville	Mar 27, 1858
Sarah B. Brown	Afton, IA	Mar 27, 1858
Nancy Walters	Brookfield	Apr 24, 1858
M. Jennie Crandall	Unadilla Forks	" " "
Nancy B. Davis	Leonardsville	May 28 "
Alonzo W. Crandall	DeRuyter	" " "
Angeline A. Stewart	Morley, MI	June 5 "
Geo. T. Crandall	Unadilla Forks	July 3, "
Luna Burdick	"	Mar 5, 1859
Josephine Clarke	"	Mar 26, "
Mary L. Hill	Bridgewater	May 6, "
Angeline Lanphere	Leonardsville	Dec 10, "
Geo. C. Stillman	"	Jan 7, 1860
Cortland N. Burch	"	Mar 17 "
Anna J. Burch	"	" " "
L. Flora Washburn	"	Jan 30, 1864
William W. Clarke	South Brookfield	" " "
Lucy J. Clarke	Cleveland, OH	" " "
Mary Caroline Crandall	Leonardsville	" " "
Jesse Burdick	Bridgewater	Sep 23, "
Nancy Babcock	Leonardsville	Mar 17, 1866
Emily A. Weaver	"	" " "
Sarah A.J. Huntley	West Winfield	" " "
Jane H. Clarke	South Brookfield	Mar 24 "
Geo. L. Whitford	Brookfield	Apr 21 "
Dea. Herman D. Clarke	New London	" " "
Frank Algerose Justus	Burlington Flatts	" " "
Mary F. Haven	Leonardsville	" " "
DeValis St. John	"	" " "
Emogene Clarke	Leonardsville	Apr 21, 1866

Alice A. Burton	Leonardsville	Apr 21, 1866
Alice M. Annis	DeRuyter	" " "
Mary L. Burch	Leonardsville	" " "
Carrie J. Lamb	West Edmeston	May 5, 1866
Mary V. Brown	Stockton, CA	May 5, 1866
Theresa M. Ellison	Leonardsville	May 26, 1866
Lucy Ann Davis	"	" " "
Rebecca E. Wheeler	"	" " "
Phebe St. John	"	" " "
Hellen V. Utter	"	" " "
Abert Whitford	"	" " "
Ruth Jane Whitford	"	" " "
Cynthia Rogers	Brookfield	" " "
Sarah Bassett	Leonardsville	" " "
Lauren B. Crandall	"	" " "
Cyrus B. Whitford	"	" " "
Mary Anthony	"	" " "
R. Biansia Church	Williamsport, PA	July 27, 1866
Eli S. Brand	Leonardsville	Oct 18, 1867
Amy Dowse	"	Nov 28, 1868
Emily D. Brown	Bridgewater	May 8, 1869
Lavina Vorden	Leonardsville	May 15, "
LeRoy Maxson	West Edmeston	May 22, "
Elizabeth Maxson	"	" " "
H. De Ette Whitford	Brookfield	" " "
Hattie L. Sisson	Leonardsville	" " "
Eliza Brown	Barry, IL	Mar 25, 1871
Ella M. Whitford	Leonardsville	" " "
E. Randall Burch	Brookfield	Apr 1, "
Morton E. Burdick	Unadulla Forks	" " "
Phebe A. Whitford	Leonardsville	" " "
Alice May St. John	Leonardsville	" " "
Clara V. Clarke	Westerly, RI	May 20, "
Charles W. Murphy	Leonardsville	Sep 20, "
Frances Murphy	"	" " "
Eld. Stephen Burdick	"	Jan 26, 1872
Susan M. Burdick	"	" " "
R. Blinn Clarke	Little Genesee	Mar 17, 1873
Cora J. Bassett	Leonardsville	" " "
Ella Meeker	Unidilla Forks	" " "
Nellie E. Hardin	Saginaw City, MI	" " "
Ora A. Searle	Unidilla Forks	" " "
Julia Marie Clarke	Leonardsville	Mar 6, 1875
Geo. Freeborn Clarke	Leonardsville	" " "
Jennie Miner	Leonardsville	" " "
Emma Wordin	Utica	Mar 13, 1875
Henry W. North	Leonardsville	" " "
Arthur C. Sisson	"	" " "
Anna M. Clarke	New London	Apr 24, "
Marilla Clarke	Leonardsville	May 22, "
Jane Bassett	"	" " "
Myra St. John	"	" " "
Eva Perkins	"	" " "
Sarah Clarke	Leonardsville	May 30, 1875

Name	Location	Date		
Sands C. Maxson	Leonardsville	Jan 17,	1876	
Estella F. Maxson	"	"	"	"
Stillman Bassett	"	Oct 7,		"
Etta Mason	"	"	"	"
G. Taylor Brown	Bridgewater	"	"	"
Mary B. Spaulding	Milton Jct., WI	dis Mar 30,	1877	
A. Malvina Graham	South Bloomfield, OH	Apr 28,		"
Irving A. Crandall	Leonardsville	"	"	"
Algerose L. Crandall	"	"	"	"
Ellen Fitch	Leonardsville	"	"	"
Henry D. Babcock	"	"	"	"
Calvin Burch	Leonardsville	"	"	"
Geno C. Rogers	"	"	"	"
Leonard J. Worden	"	"	"	"
Alle A. Whitford	"	"	"	"
Mamie E. Whitford	"	"	"	"
Mattie J. Sisson	"	"	"	"
Periz R. Brownell	West Winfield	"	"	"
Nora B. Jennings	Brookfield	"	"	"
M. Julia Stillman	Leonardsville	"	"	"
Lucy Jane Edwards	"	"	"	"
Ann C. Brownell	West Winfield	May 26,	1877	
Cornelia J. Wells	Leonardsville	Sep 28,		"
Clark M. Bassett	Leonardsville	Mar 30,	1878	
Adda L. Brown	"	"	"	"
Hattie E. Babcock	"	"	"	"
Annette M. Bass	"	July 26,	1878	
Wm. H. Brand	"	Sep 14,		"
Fidelia D. Champlin	"	Mar 29,	1879	
Lizzie B. King	"	"	"	"
Silas Clapson	West Winfield	Jan 31,	1880	
Jane W. Clapson	"	"	"	"
Minnie Clapson	"	May 29,		"
H. Isabell Brand	Leonardsville	Mar 31,	1882	
Jesse Clarke	"	Apr 8,		"
Emily H. Davis	"	"	"	"
Darwin S. Crandall	"	"	"	"
Alzina Crandall	"	"	"	"
Geo. A. Rogers	Brookfield	"	"	"
Oatly W. Wells	Leonardsville	"	"	"
Roscoe C. Worden	"	"	"	"
Charles F. Maxson	"	"	"	"
Edgar Mason	"	"	"	"
Alvira Adams	"	"	"	"
M. Josie Brownell	West Winfield	"	"	"
Agnes E. Babcock	Leonardsville	"	"	"
Emily L. Burdick	"	Apr 29,	1882	
Arthur W. Crandall	"	May 13,		"
Elvah Crandall	"	"	"	"
Celia Rogers	"	"	"	"

Primary Sorces are in poor condition; it seemed wiser to type from the Manual of 1883. IMS:1993

SECOND BROOKFIELD
Located in Brookfield, Madison Co.; organized 1823

The first record book is not extant so a paper written by Rev. Walter L. Greene with notes by Ruby Clarke Todd (Mrs. C.M.) is used. They quote from the old record book.

Constituent Members

Joshua Wells	Charles Babcock
Welcome Babcock	Andrew Babcock
Sam L. Babcock	Ira Spencer
Sanders Langworthy	Augustus Saunders
William Franklin	Paul Clarke
Jonathan Babcock	Mercy Langworthy
Richard Clarke	Henry Danford
Martha Kellogg	Joseph Langworthy, Jr.
Sylva Bentley	Solomon Barnes
Celesta Langworthy	James Perkins
Anna Lewis	Tacy Babcock
Elias L. Langworthy	Emma Langworthy
Robert L. Davis	Elisa Wells
Tacy Babcock	Christopher Langworthy
Eli S. Bailey	Silas Spencer
Lois Langworthy	Belina Wells

SECOND RECORD BOOK   SECOND BROOKFIELD

The second record is extant but is in poor condition, badly cut up and illegible in spots. It contains a list of clerks, contributers, and some minutes.

List of Comtributers
1837

Henry Holmes	Seth Holmes $25
Chester Palmiter $20	Ethan Stillman
Richard Stillman	Asa Frink $20
Silas Bailey $20	Eli S. Bailey $20
Joshua Bruce $20.50	Saunders Langworthy $15
Wait Clarke $15	Leroy Murphy $13
Varnum Gorton $15	Phineas Babcock $20
Benjamin Burdick $20	H.B. Clarke $10.35
John Hibbard $25	Stanton Burdick $20.50
Abel Palmer $20.56	Solomon Gorton $22
Andrew Babcock $4.98	Kilburn Crandall $25
Clark M. Whitford $24	James Crandall $2.50
J. Brand $20.50	D. B. Brinkly $30.
J. T. Crandall $32.50	Phineas Babcock $.19.93

1838

Hona B. Clark $3.75	W. A. Denison $10
H. B. Clark $13.25	Benjamin Gorton $10

Bell Lewis $28
Charles Foster $31
Benjamin Burdick, Jr. $20
M. E. Babcock $20
Jonathan Babcock $25.38
Silas Bailey $13.26
William Greene $16.14
Charles Foote $13.16
Abel Palmer $7.44
Kilburn Crandall $25

David Hinkley $25
Luther Hinkley $20
D. Randall $5
B. Yortors $10
John Doolittle $10
Charles Foster $13.60
Wait Burdick $20
Benjamin Gorton $1
J. Hibbard $12
Charles Foster $ 13.60

1839

Wait Burdick $5.69
R. Stillman $50
Andrew Babcock $49.52
Rawsor Babcock $20
James Hills $16. 50 in 1837
Adin Burdick $24
James Denison $40

E. Stillman $ 50.
Samual H. Coon $14.98
J.T.G. Bailey $29
J. D. Denison $20
Dewitt Coon $14.98
Aratt. Hills $26

1840

Jonathon Babcock $ 25.62
Wait Clarke $ 13.82

Oliver C. Brown $32.22
Robert Burdick $14.26

1841

R. Stillman $51

The above list was typed from the second record book of 2nd Brookfield. CRR 19x.13 vault.

IMS:1993

RECORD BOOK of THIRD BROOKFIELD SDB CHURCH organized 1823
WEST EDMESTON
Edmeston Twsp., Otsego Co., NY

p. 4 " Eighty names were enrolled at formation of the church as shown by the following list of members."

Daniel Coon
Joshua Maxson
Elias Burdick
Adin Burdick
Desire Burdick d/o Elisha
David Maxson
Martha Burdick w/o Rows B.
Prudence Stillman w/o Benjamin
Isaac W. Brown
James Crandall
Joel Maxson
Peleg Babcock
Ephraim Maxson
Henry M. Crandall
Saunders Crandall
Joseph S. Crandall
Rachel Maxson w/o Joel
Betsey Crumb w/o Silas
Sarah Burdick w/o Charles
Hannah Burdick w/o David

Samuel B. Crandall
Samuel P. Burdick
Lydia Burdick wid/o Elisha
Benjamin Burdick
Thankful Maxson w/o Joshua
Lydia Champlin w/o George C.
Sarah Burdick w/o Robert
Nathan Stillman
Ethan R. Crandall
Augustus Crandall
Nathan Burch
John Maxson
Danas Chapin
Franklin Coon
Rowland Coon
Thankful Crandall w/o James
Polly Crandall w/o Sanders
Fanny Stillman w/o Nathan
Olive Crandall w/o James S.
Nancy Clarke d/o Luke

p. 5
Prudence Clarke d/o Luke
Clarissa Babcock w/o Ephraim
Polly Burdick w/o Samuel P.
Damaris Burch w/o Nathan
Fanny Coon w/o Daniel
Sally Coon w/o Rowland
Mary Edwards w/o Benjamin
Amy Coon w/o Abram
Elizabeth Brown w/o J. W.
Alvira Maxson w/o John
Charles Potter
Olive Coon w/o Samuel H.
Ezra Coon
Eliza Potter w/o Charles
Kenyon Crandall
Caleb Church
Ethan Stillman
Betsey Nye w/o B. B. Nye
Luke Clarke
Patty Babcock w/o Charles B., Jr.

Phebe Babcock d/o Jonathan
Thankful Crandall w/o Aldrich
Savinia Maxson d/o Joel
Nancy Babcock w/o Jonathan
Lucy Griswold
Benjamin Edwards
Abram Coon
Anna Coon d/o Abram
Philestra Crandall w/o Ethan
Daniel Brown
Samuel H. Coon
Joshua Maxson, Jr
Mary Burdick d/o Samuel P.
Fanny Wilbur
Mary Crandall w/o Kenyon
Esther Church
Weeden Witter
Mary Crandall d/o James
Cysene Coon w/o Ezra
Ephraim Clarke

"After fifteen years it was found that a majority of the members had become located in and around West Edmeston and for their accomadation, they built a chapel in 1843."

p. 8
"Names of Excluded Members Previous to Loss of Records"

    Masion Denison
    Flosus C. Bassett   Amanda J. Odell-Sabbath Breaking

p. 9
"Names of Deceased Members Previous to Loss of Records"

NAME	Date	AGE
Kenyon Crandall	Dec 22, 1866	82
Mary Crandall	Feb 8, 1880	
Betsey Holt		
Benjamin Stillman	Oct 22, 1881	88
Maria J. Holt		
Amos Stillman	1878	
Abigail Millard Coon		
Dea. Ephraim Maxson	April 5, 1872	72
Phebe Crandall		
Herman A. Hull		
Mrs. Herman A. Hull		
Dwight Pardee	April 23, 1879	
Aurilla Coon	Feb 24, 1877	68
Ezra Coon		
Hannah Farbush		
Margaret Crandall		
Joshua Maxson	Sep 29, 1873	
Anna D. Maxson	Aug 27, 1871	
Benjamin Burdick	Jul 25, 1876	80
Mrs. Benjamin Burdick	April 15, 1877	80

p. 10

NAMES	DESIGNATION	MEMBERSHIP CEASED	REMARKS
Rev. J. B. Clarke,	Pastor	Feb. 9, 1890	by letter
Eunice S. "	w/o J.B.C.	Aug 1, 1888	"
William R. "	s/o "	Sep 8, 1882	"
Alvord B. "	" "	Aug 1, 1888	"
Myna S. "	d/o "	May 14, 1892	"
John S. Coon- b. Jan. 21, 1807		Mar. 26, 1891	death
bequest: $500 to church			
Martha E. Coon	w/o J.S.		death
Linnus Pardee		Dec 29, 1880	"
Betsey "	w/o Linnus	Jan 2, 1896	"
Emeliza "	d/o "	July 5, 1927	"
Adelaide Pardee Seale	d/o "	April 10, 1927	"
Samuel Dresser		March 14, 1887	"
Betsey "	w/o Samuel	Oct 14, 1880	"
Phebe L. Bassett	w/o Clarke B. (dec.);	June 21, 1883	"
William H. "	s/o "	Nov 12, 1887	"
Catharine Champlin	w/o Jeffrey C.	1892	"
Catharine "	d/o " "	1904	"
Adelaid Champlin Denison	d/o J.C.	Dec 31, 1898	"

Name	Date	Notes
Martha Coon d/o Ezra C.	Sep 4, 1907	"
Ransom Brown	Jan. 25, 1892	"
Zeruah Maxson w/o Dea. Ephraim	Aug. 9, 1883	"

p. 12

Name	Date	Notes
William M. Palmiter-age 68	June 4, 1889	"
Phebe Palmiter w/o William P. d/o E. Maxson	July 30, 1892 age 65	"
Adolph Nichols	April 21, 1914	"
Ruben H. White	Jan 6, 1892	"
Maria E. " w/o Ruben age: 75 yrs. 5 mo. 9 days	July 24, 1914	"
C. Kerrie Burdick s/o William H. b. 1858	Nov 26, 1887	letter
Eliza J. Burdick w/o Kerrie	Nov 26, 1887	"
Benjamin Stillman-age: 88 yrs.	Oct 22, 1887	death
Variety Green Stillman w/o Benj.	Dec 31, 1880	"
William H. Burdick	Mar 31, 1888	letter
Elizabeth Stillman Burdick w/o Wm. H.	Mar 31, 1888	"
Carlton H. Burdick s/o W.H. Burdick	June 25, 1888	"
William B. Stillman s/o Benjamin		death
Susan Holt Stillman	Sep 13, 1886	"
Eunice Crandall-b. 1807 age: 90 yrs	May 8, 1896	"
Amelia Crandall Perry d/o Mrs. Susan Crandall	Mar 1, 1891	Excom.
Alanson C. Potter		letter
Mary S. Burdick Potter w/o A. C. Potter	June 1905	death
Judith Potter Crandall	1905	death
Henry P. Crandall	June 14, 1884	death
Mariam E. Crandall w/o Henry	Nov 17, 1895	Excom.
Jennie E. Humphrey	Mar 25, 1894	"

p. 14

Name	Date	Notes
Franklin F. McGrew	Dec 18, 1881	"
Rosa Robins " w/o F.F. McGrew	Mar 4, 1883	"
Mary McIntyre Bennett	June 3, 1900	"
Elizabeth Barker w/o Macomber B.	1904	death
Eunice Millard w/o J.B. Millard b. Jan 28, 1828	July 21, 1912	"
Rhoda S. Maxson d/o David b. Feb 27, 1844	Mar 15, 1910	"
Abbie Whittemore Millard-b. Mar 14, 1858 adopted d/o J.B.M.		letter to Scot, NY
Jane Whittemore Millard w/o D. Millard b. July 28, 1856	May 17, 1888	death
Eunice Burdick Stillman w/o Amos b. Jan 12, 1835	Aug 1, 1919	"
Daniel S. Maxson	1903	"
Louisa Maxson w/o Daniel	Nov 14, 1906	"
Weathy Burdick Felton	Feb 12, 1882	"
Ransom T. Stillman	July 22, 1889	"
Eunice E. Stillman w/o R.T.S.	May 17, 1888	"
Charles Stillman s/o R.T.S.	Feb 15, 1911	2nd Brookfield

Eliza A. Stillman d/o R.T.S.
Hattie M. Stillman d/o R.T.S.
Saunders Crandall-b. Aug 12, 1786   Jan 27, 1880   death
Morell Coon-age: 79 yrs   Nov 8, 1913   "
Emmar B. Coon w/o Morell   Feb 1925   "
Almeron M. Coon s/o "   Mar 20, 1890 1st Brookfield

p. 16
Franklin E. Dresser- b. June 19, 1827   June 30, 1923   95 yrs
Pallis Hooker Dresser w/o Franklin   April 14, 1914 84 yrs
Alice A. Dresser Peet d/o Franklin   Jan 19, 1895 1st Brookfield
Bethiah Crandall Welch   July 2, 1884   death
Harrison W. Gates   June 22, 1921   "
Sarah Ann Gates w/o Harrison   Mar   1927   "
Eudora Gates Welch d/o "   Jan 15, 1898 1st Brookfield
Berdell Gates s/o Harrison   June 3, 1888   Excom.
Truman H. Maxson   May 15, 1893   death
Lynn C. Maxson s/o Truman   no date
Cornelia Crumb Clarke   no date   death
Alonzo B. Felton   Feb 21, 1911   death
Adelaide Brooks Felton w/o Alonzo   Feb 14, 1921   "
Elbert A. Felton s/o Alonzo   no date
Justin Reed   Dec 3, 1882   Excom.
Arches Reed w/o Justin   Nov 1, 1891   death
Willard Sarabee   May 2, 1892   letter
Olive Burdick w/o David B.   Nov 18, 1887   death
Nathaniel Sprague   1905   "
Sovisa Sprague w/o Nathaniel; dis Dec 1914 Leonardsville; d. May 30'21
Cornelia Burch Brand-dis by letter to 2nd Brookfield   no date

p. 18
Martha Crandall Brown   June 5, 1887   Excom.
Thomas T. Burdick-b. Feb 5, 1842   Nov 4, 1902   Alfred, NY
Harriett V. Douse Burdick w/o Thomas   Nov 4, 1902   "   "
     b. Mar 18, 1842
Mary Crandall w/o Kenyon, (dec.)   Feb 8, 1880   death
John Henry Burch-b. June 20, 1815   Apr 23, 1900   "
     our oldest member
Phebe Hinkley Burch w/o J.H.B.   July 31, 1885   "
Mary Abbie Burch Burdick d/o J.H.B.   Jan 31, 1891 1st Brookfield
David Burch s/o J.H.B.   death
Anna Flemming Burch w/o David
Nathan Burch s/o J.H.B.   Dec 24, 1881 2nd Brookfield
Mary Chapman Burch w/o Nathan   Sep   1881   death
Susan Wilcox w/o Amos; 84 yrs   Oct 1, 1882   "
Lucy P. Crandall w/o Ira B.   July 4, 1882   "
Ira J. Ordway   Sep 8, 1883   Chicago
Eliza A. Ordway w/o Ira   "   "   "   "
Albert K. Ordway s/o Ira   Mar 2, 1884   Excom.
Henry C. Babcock   Mar 29, 1892   death
Harriet M. Babcock w/o Henry   Mar 30, 1885   "
William A. Crandall- b. Dec. 1831; 88yrs Aug 18, 1919   "
Clarrisa Crandall w/o William   Jan 22, 1887   "
Hannah Clarke Van Dee   Dec 19, 1880   Excom.

p. 20
Daniel Brown	Dec 8, 1883	death
Mrs. Daniel Brown(Abigail Langworthy) b. Oct 29, 1805	Mar 24, 1882	"
Mary Este Burdick	Nov 26, 1878	"
Halsey H. Williams	no date	"
Lucetta Williams w/o Halsey	May 1926	
Albertus Clarke	June 3, 1900	Excom.
Leila Clarke d/o Henry Clarke	Mar 24, 1894	"
John J. Hull	June 5, 1887	"
Anna Hull w/o John J.	" " "	"

Herbert Clifford Brown-ad Dec 31, 1881;   Mar 9, 1888   2nd Brookfield
Caroline Babcock Brown w/o Herbert-ad Dec. 31, 1881; dis Mar 9, 1888
Emily Burdick-dis 1st Brookfield   Apr 29, 1882
Lizzie Babcock Maxson w/o Coridon S.-ad Aug 4, 1883;   EXCOM 1914
Orson Champlin-bp. Oct 6, 1883   Dec 15, 1900   death
Cora G. Nichols w/o Adolph Nichols-bp Oct 6, 1883;   d. July 18, 1917
Eda R. Coon Maxson d/o Morell & Emmar-bp Nov 22, 1884;dis Nov 21'91 Farina
Lucius H. Burdick s/o WM & Elizabeth-bp Nov 22,1884
           dis. by letter to 1st Brookfield Mar. 31, 1888
Esther E. Williams-letter to Plainfield, NJ Feb. 20, 1897
Cartha Williams Rollins-adopted dau of Halsie;bp Feb 14,1885; EXCOM
Emmett J. Williams-bp Feb 14, 1885;   June 1, 1890   Excom.
Frederick H. White-bp " " "   July 27, 1936   death

P. 22
Bertha M. Stillman Dresser d/o Amos and Eunice;bp & ad Feb 14, 1885
Charles D. Coon-s/o George & Cordelia- bp & ad Feb 14, 1885
         dis by letter to 1st Brookfield   Mar 20, 1890
Grace E. Coon see entry above
Nettie A. Coon see entry above
Clara M. Coon See entry above
Nancy S. Corbett Stillman d/o John Corbett; bp & ad Feb 21, 1885
         dis by letter to 2nd Brookfield   Jan. 12, 1901
Mary M. Corbett d/o John Corbett-bp & ad Feb 21, 1885;Excom Nov 26,'99
Sua M.Clarke d/o Eld J. B.-bp & ad Feb 21, 1885; dis Aug 1,'88 1st Alfred
Reuben T. Crandall s/o Wm A.-bp & ad Feb 21, 1855;   Excom Jun 1, 1890
Lillie S. Crandall Card d/o Wm. A.-bp & ad Feb 21, 1885   EXCOM
Rev. Clayton A. Burdick, Pastor-ad Oct 17, 1885;
         dis. by letter to pastor 2nd Brookfield May 11, 1889
Francis B. Sprague Austin d/o of Nathaniel-bp & ad Oct 24, 1885
         Excom. Mar. 28, 1897 Disregard of Covenent & Sabbath
Sarah M. Gates Tolbok d/o Harrison-bp & ad Oct. 24, 1885
         Excom. Mar. 26, 1899 Disregard of Covenent & Sabbath
Amelia E. White d/o Reuben-b. May 12, 1863;bp & ad Jun 5,'86; d. no date
LeRoy Maxson s/o John-ad Apr 14, 1888   d. Dec. 23, 1901
Elizabeth Maxson w/o Leroy-ad Apr 14, 1888;dis May 19, 1906 Leonardsville
Flora Crandall Cutler w/o Levi-d/o Susan Crandall; bp & ad Sep 15, 1888
             dis. by letter to Chicago   Jan. 1893
Rev. Alphonso Lawrence, Pastor-ad Apr 13, 1889;   dis 1893 Berlin
Emma A. Lawrence see entry above
Zarria Sholes Felton w/o E.A. Felton-ad Jan 4, 1890; d. Aug. 16, 1930

p. 24
Lester D. Burdick s/o T.T. & H.V.D.-b. May 22, 1874; dis Nov Nov 4,1902 Alfred
   bp Oct. 4, 1890
Herbert I. Burdick s/o T.T.& H.V.D.-b. Jun 23,1875; bp Oct 4, 1890;
       dis letter to Alfred Nov. 4, 1902
Mary A. Burdick d/o T.T. & H.V.D.-b. Jun 1,1877; bp Oct 4, 1890;
       dis Nov 4, 1902 Alfred
George A. Burdick s/o T.T.& H.V.D-b. Jul 6,1879; bp Oct 4, 1890
       dis letter to Alfred Nov. 4, 1902
Rev. Martin Sindall, Pastor s/o C. J. Sindall-b. Jul 25,1867
   ad Aug. 19, 1893; dis Sep 14, 1895 1st Verona
Cora Belle Sindall w/o see above entry
Edith C. Burch d/oNathan Burch-bp Aug 1893; d. Jan 22, 1900
  Bap. Aug.,1893; death: Jan. 22, 1900
Mary Burch Ray d/o Nathan Burch-bp Aug 1893
    Excom. for disregard of Covenent & Sabbath no date
Nathan Burch, Jr. s/o Nathan Burch see above entry
Minnie B. Stillman w/o Wm. B. Stillman-bp Sep 16, 1893; d. Jul 31, 1916
Anna W. Maxson w/o Truman H. Maxson-bp Sep 16, 1893 d. no date
Mrs. Alice Marie Buell-bp Mar 9, 1895 EXCOM no date
Maggie Millard Hosie, b. Sep. 5, 1882; bp May 1895
    dis Little Genesee, NY Jun. 27,1914
George Buel-bp Aug 31, 1895; Excom. Sabbath breaking no date
Rev. Madison Harry, Pastor-ad Apr 24, 1891; dis Westerly no date
Esther Williams Harry-ad from Plainfield Jan 20, 1900; d. Aug 1933
Mary Williams, mother of Esther W. Harry formerly of Watson, NY
  b. Nov.25, 1829; ad Jan 20, 1900 d. 1922
Ray R. Williams s/o Mary Williams - b. July 6, 1860; d. May 13, 1932
  ad from Watson: Jan 20, 1900;
Addie A. Williams Zarrabee d/o Mary Williams - b. Dec 7, 1870
  ad from Watson: Jan 20, 1900; d. 1928
Lydia L. Williams Mayes d/o Mary Williams - b. Dec 5, 1867
  ad from Watson Jan 20, 1900
Martha M. Williams d/o Mary Williams - b. Oct 13, 1873 d. 1914
  ad letter from Watson Jan 13, 1900

p. 26
Laurentine Stephens-b. May 20, 1864; ad Jan. 20, 1900
Ida Eudora Stephens w/o of Laurentine - b. May 2, 1867; ad Jan 20,1900
Henry F. Burdick - bp Feb 3, 1900; d. Mar 23, 1903
Irving Crandall s/o L.B. Crandall - bp Feb 3, 1900; EXCOM ad 1st day church
Lauren B. Crandall f/o Irving - bp Feb 3, 1900; d. Jan 24, 1917
Howard Harry s/o Rev. Madison Harry - bp Feb 3, 1900; d. Oct 10, 1920
Mary E. White w/o Fred H. White - b. Nov 12, 1871; bp Feb 3, 1900
Jessie Myrtle Stephen Augell d/o Laurentine -b. Jun 13, 1885; bp Aug 24,1901
Mabel Caroline Stephens Risley - b. Apr 1887; ad Aug 24, 1901
A. C. Davis, Jr. M. D. - ad Sep 15, 1900; d. accidental May 4, 1908
Carrie E. Davis w/o A. C. Davis - ad May 4, 1901; dis no date
Julua Maxson w/o Lynn C. Maxson - ad May 4, 1901
Lizzie M. Holmes - ad Aug 24, 1901; Excom.
Bessie M. Nicholes d/o Adolph N. - ad Aug 24, 1901; d. 1904
Mrs. Harriet Stone - ad Jan 17, 1903;
  EXCOM going back to 1st Baptist Church Sep 22, 1919

Edmon F. Davis - ad from Watson Jan 24, 1903
Evelyn Young Davis w/o Edmon-ad from Watson Feb 4, 1903
Hattie Crandall w/o Bryon - ad Feb 14, 1903
Marie L. McIntyre w/o Almon - bp June 27, 1903; d. 1921
Anna Williams Beldon d/o Lucetta - bp Jul 4, 1903; d. Oct 10, 1920

p. 28
Miss Sarah Seale gd/o Elizabeth - ad Jul 4,1903; dis May 1906 Leonardsville
Miss Zella Stephens d/o Lauentine - bp Jul 27, 1903
Floyd L. Larabee s/o Bret - bp Jun 27, 1903
Lamont Stillman s/o R.F.S. - ad from 1st Brookfield; dis Verona   no dates
Nettie Stillman w/o Lamont - ad from 1st Brookfield Jul 18, 1903 dis Verona
Mrs. Cornelia M. Babcock -ad from 1st Utica Presbyterian Church Nov 17, 1906
                    d. Oct 18, 1822
Miss Hattie White d/o Fred H. - bp Aug 10, 1807; d. Jun 5, 1824
Ernest White s/o Fred H. - bp Aug 10, 1907; ad NY Church
Fannie Larabee Monroe d/o Bert L. - bp Aug 10, 1907; dis Oct 4, 1925
Walter Crandall - bp Aug 10, 1907; dis. Oct 10, 1920
Elva Larabee Crandall d/o Brayton - bp Aug 10, 1907
                         dis to 2nd Brookfield Oct. 10, 1920
Brayton Larabee - ad Aug 10,1907
Sarah Larabee w/o Brayton - ad Aug 10, 1907
Abbie M. Burdick w/o Grant - ad from Scot Mar 1909
Grant Burdick - b. Sep 1, 1852; ad from DeRuyter Mar 1909;
                          d. Mar 22, 1923
Rev. Riley G. Davis-dis. to Syracuse 1911
Mrs. R. G. Davis   "   "   "   "
Meredith Maxson-bp Sep 7, 1912; dp joined 1st day church Oct 10, 1920
Maud Dresser - bp Sep 7, 1912
Mabel   "   "   "   "
Leslie Larrabee - bp. Sep 7, 1912

p. 30
Herbert Lewis Polan, Pastor - ad Aug 3,1912; dis Oct 5, 1912
Adeline A. Polan   see above entry
Rev. Alonzo G. Crofoot, Pastor - ad Dec 5, 1914
      dis. to pastor Marlboro June 1, 1917
Lena G. Crofoot w/o Alonzo   see above entry
Lamont Stillman - ad Aug 7, 1915; d. Mar 5, 1937
Rev. Leon D. Burdick, Pastor - ad Jul 21, 1917; dis Jun 1, 1919
Nellie Burdick w/o L.D.   see above entry
Mrs. Lena G. Crofoot, Pastor, - ad Nov 15, 1919; dis Nov 1, 1928
Fred C. Langworthy - ad Jan 17, 1920; d. no date
Edwina Langworthy w/o Fred - ad Jan 17, 1920
Althea Langworthy d/o Fred - ad Jan 17, 1920
Newell Welch - bp Aug 31, 1929

West Edmeston SDB Church Records 1823-1844
CRR 19x.26 Vault   IMS:1993

DeRuyter, Madison Co., NY
first organized 1806

Membership in 1806

At German now Lincklaen	at DeRuyter
Joseph Saunders	Benjamin Burdick
Joseph Stillman	John Beebet
Thomas Stillman	Matthew Wells, Jr.
John Maxson	Horace Greene
Lucy Burdick	Debora Johnson
Temperance Coon	Elizabeth Wells
Elizabeth Coon	Polly Beebe
Elizabeth Maxson	Elizabeth Johnson, Jr.
Olive Saunders	Polly Maxson
Welthy Burdick	Elias Wells
Caty Burdick	Phanny Wells
Sylvia Burdick	Mrs. Phanny Wells

David Davis: 1st pastor

"In Nov. 1810 the DeRuyter Church was received as a branch of the Berlin Church. At the reorganization in 1816, Berlin dismissed the following members."

Henry Burdick	David Wells
William Coon	Hannah Coon
Polly Coon	Betsey Burdick
David Burdick	Nancy Burdick
Thomas Burdick	Temperance Burdick

MS 1967.10.9   B-file
The author states he got the material from Berlin records.
IMS:1993

REORGANIZATION: 1816

" Names of persons who have been held in membership in the SDB Church of DeRuyter since Sept. 15, 1815."

Names	From	Names	From
James Coon	RI	William Saunders	Hopkinton
Jared Stillman	Berlin	Hannah Coon	DeRuyter
Thomas Stillman	"	George Burdick	DeRuyter
Joshua Stillman	"	Thompson Burdick	"
Joseph Stillman	"	Avis Coon	"
Abigail Stillman	"	Nancy Coon	Berlin
Betsey Stillman	"	Catherine Coon	"
Sally Stillman	"	Solomon Coon	"
Elizabeth Wells	"	Elizabeth Maxson	"
Catharine Wells	"	Silva Burdick	"
Olive Saunders	DeRuyter	Weden Burdick	DeRuyter

Elizabeth Wells, Jr. "
Kenyon Burdick Hopkinton
John Greene   Hopkinton
Betsey Greene   "
Rowland T. Greene   "
Joanna Greene   "
Nancy Coon   Hopkinton
Henry C. Burdick Berlin
Betsey Burdick   "
Esther Burdick   "
Fanny Wells   "
Samuel Stillman, Jr. Berlin
Grace Stillman   Berlin
Samuel Greenman   "
Betsey Crumb   Brookfield
Lucy Burdick   Berlin
Zachery Maxson Hopkinton
Charlotte Nichols DeRuyter
Luke Coon   Berlin
Rolly Beebe   "
Temperance Burdick DeRuyter
Matthew Wells   Berlin
"   "   Jr.   "
Welthea   "   "
David   "   "
John B. Stillman Hopkinton
Elisha   "   "
Alpheus M. Green   "
Caleb W. Church   "
Abby Greene   "
Avis Coon d/o Luke DeRuyter
Eli Colegrove   Brookfield
Annis Coon   DeRuyter
Jonathan Bentley
Polly Burdick
Benjamin C. Maxson Hopkinton
Martha Maxson   "
Luke Clarke
Aaron Fox
Prudence Crandall
Sally Hamilton
Esther Muncy
Jermiah Cotrell   Scott
Polly Lamphier
D. Betsey Burdick
Avis Coon
Nathan Might
Susan Irish
Hannah Simmons
Enoch Maxson
Maria Irish   Hopkinton
Emily Maxson
Henry Crandall, Jr Berlin
Olive Richmond   "

Rosewell Richmond   "
Thomas H. Burdick Berlin
Samuel Stillman   "
Lydia Stillman   "
Elisha Stillman   "
Elma Maxson   "
Elias Wells   "
Hannah Coon   "
Pruda Coon   "
William Coon   "
Deadamie Coon   "
Temperance Coon   "
Emily Nichols   "
Jared Maxson   "
Luke Burdick   Brookfield
Hannah Burdick   DeRuyter
Elizabeth Oviat   Berlin
Lydia Crandall   "
Lydia Coon   "
Thankful Richmond DeRuyter
Abigail Lewis   Hopkinton
Henry Olin   Genesee
Lucy Olin   "
Benjamin Burdick   Berlin
Sylvester Crumb Brookfield
Elias Irish   Hopkinton
Martha Sheldon   "
Rush Crumb   Brookfield
Betsey "   "
Polly Church   Hopkinton
Susan Kenyon   "
Laura Olin
Judith Bentley
Barber Cardson
Polly   "
Judith Coleman Brookfield
Zacheus R. Maxson
Anna Clarke
Chloe Fox
Seymour Hamilton
James Muncy
Cynthia Might
Sally Cotrell   Scott
Lydia S. Babcock   "
Maria Colegrove
Parley Cory
Jacob Simmons
Olive Coy
Perry Burdick
Eli S. Colegrove, Jr.
Malvina Colegrove
Virtue Maxson
Esther Crandall
Pardon Coon

Polly Maxson
Elisha Wells
Daniel B. Coon
Lydia Stillman
Asa C. Nichols
Betsey "
Russel G. Burdick
Martha Burdick
Barbara Cardner, Jr
Mary "
Horace Church
Jason Burdick
Sally Pye
Benjamin Maxson
Levi Coy
Matthew W. Crandall
Thomas Pye
Polly Cardner
Crynus Cartwright, Jr.
Betsey Burdick   Berlin
Wid. Rebecca Maxson   Scott
William Stewaet Maxson   "
Benjamin H. Burdick   Berlin
George Burdick
Lorrna Stillman
Salina Stillman
Eunice Olin
Clarke Coon
Deborah Coon
Maxson Stillman
Eunice Coon
Jonathan Coon
Avza Coon
Hannah Colegrove
Phineas Burdick
Clarinda Green
William G. Crandall
Esther Coon
Alonzo Coon
Cornelia Burdick
Sally Olin
Thomas H. Burdick
Darwin S. Crandall
Susannah Cartwright
Abel A. C. Sanders
Lydia Champlin   3rd Brookfield
Esther Stillman   Berlin
Emma Stillman
Lydia Burdick
Esther Burdick
Julia Ann Burdick
Mary Breed
Luke Coon, Jr.
Albert Burdick

Abigail Stillman
Avery Coon
Alanson P. Stillman
Millia Potter
Eliza Burdick
Vernam M. Burdick
Luanna   "
Mary Irish
Daniel C. Richmond
Pricilla   "
John Dye
Mary Pye
Anna "
Isaac Phillips
William Allen
John Pye
David Cardner
Lucinda Burdick
Daniel Burdick   Berlin
Polly Coon   Scott
Amy Maxson   "
Susannah Maxson "
Hannah Burdick   Berlin
Lucy Burdick
Robert Stillman
Hannah Cartwright
Lucy Maxson
Adelia Stillman
Eunice Maxson
Esther Coon
Ferrissa Coon
Ambrose Coon
Lydia Crandall
Martha Colegrove
Lois Coon
Aurilla Iraman
Abram Coon
Celinda L. Olin
Seberus M. Burdick
Emeline Champlin
Sheffield B. Maine
William Crandall
William Cartwright
Diana Nichols
Alonzo H. Burdick
Almeda Burdick
Emily H. Maine
Martha Stillman
Maria Burdick
Polly Burdick
Mary Sanders
Almira Coon
Polly Lesure

Jason B. Wells - bp July, 1831
Kenyon Burdick
Henry C. Babcock - fr 2nd Brookfield
Matthew W. Williams - fr 2nd Brookfield
Julia Ann McKey - bp 1832
Wilborn S. Wells - bp; d. Sep 1843
Lucius Crandall - fr 2nd Brookfield 1932
Luke P. Babcock - fr Scott   Dec 1832
Lydia Babcock   "   "   "   "
Temperance Babcock - bp 1832
Hampton S. Bently - fr Scott 1833
Amos Colegrove - bp 1833
Esther Church -bp- Nov 23, 1833
Betsey Crumb - fr Otselic 1833
John Freeman - fr Scott Apr 1834
Stephen Maxson - fr Lincklaen   Apr 1834
Jared Crandall - fr 2nd Brookfield Apr 1834
Lydia Crandall   "   "   "   "
Maria Holcomb - fr Scott Apr 1834
Mary Freman -bp by Elder Crandall
Cynthia Freman - fr Scott; d. Oct 8, 1835
Wid. Anna Davis - fr Preston
Albert Stillman - bp May 10, 1834
Anna Crumb - fr Otselic
Eld. Alexander Campbell - fr Truxton Mar 10, 1834
Oliver Crandall - fr Hopkinton
Katharine Maxson - fr Berlin
Mary Church w/o Caleb; fr Truxton
Susan Church - fr Truxton
Artemas Coon - bp Sep 20, 1834
Clarripa Leins - ad Sep 20, 1834; d. Aug 1832
Halsey H. Baker - bp Oct 25, 1834
Elizabeth Williams - fr Berlin   Oct 1834
Clarinda Campbell - fr Truxton
Alonzo W. Crandall - bp Nov 1834
Arvilla E. Crandall   "   "   "
Ellen Babcock   "   "   "
Thomas Coon   "   "   "
Susan Coon - fr Truxton Nov 1834
Franklin Coon - bp 1834
Caroline Coon   "   "
Martha W. Richmond - bp 1834
Ezra Burdick - fr Truxton
Caleb W. Church - fr Truxton
Gaylord Maxson - bp Dec 6, 1834
Hiram S. Crandall - bp Jan 19, 1835
Eaton Pulford - ad Jan 19, 1835
Elias Wells - bp "   "   "   ; d. Aug 12, 1843
Joseph Clarke Crandall - d. Aug 12, 1843
Elizabeth Crandall - d. Aug 12, 1843
Katharine Crumb - bp Jan 19, 1835
Juliaette Wells - bp Jan 17, 1833; d. Oct 10, 1843
Sally Coon - bp Jul 17, 1835
Esther Richmond

Horace Church - fr Truxton
Alonzo H. Burdick - fr Schenectady; rejected Oct, 1837
Betsey Burdick - fr Lincklaen
Perry Burdick - fr Lincklaen
Lucy Burdick - fr Lincklaen
David Babcock - fr Scott Sep 26, 1835
Elmira Babcock   "   "   "   "   "
Mary Ann Church - fr Truxton
Bethuel C. Church - fr Petersburg May, 1836
William Maxson - fr Hopkinton Aug 1836
Sarah Maxson - fr Waterford CN Nov 4, 1836
Solomon Carpenter - fr Berlin Jul 21, 1837
Sally Stewart - fr Persia NY
Lucy M. Clark w/o S. Carpenter - fr 2nd Brookfield Nov 11, 1837
Dea. John Maxson - fr Schenectady Dec 2, 1837
Mary Maxson - fr Schenectady Dec 2, 1837
Caleb Maxson - fr Schenectady Dec 2, 1837
Mary Maxson w/o Caleb - fr Schenectady Dec 2, 1837
Cornelia P. Maxson - fr Schenectady Dec 2, 1837
William D. Cockran - fr Clarence 1837
Ransom F. Stillman - fr 2nd Hopkinton 1837
Barton G. Stillman -   "   "   "
Caroline B. Maxson - fr Schenectady
Dea. Samuel P. Burdick - fr 3rd Brookfield
Polly Burdick w/o S. P. B.; fr 3rd Brookfield
Mary Burdick - fr 3rd Brookfield
Saphronia Burdick - fr 3rd Brookfield
Sarah Burdick - fr 3rd Brookfield
Catharine Euphemia Cockran
Marcia Carpenter - bp Jan 1838
Clark Burdick -   "   "   "
Daniel Coon -   "   "   "
H. Sophronia Wells - bp by Eld. Campbell
Cornelia Crandall -   "   "   "   "
Benjamin Scrivens -   "   "   "   "
Ann Dowse - fr 3rd Brookfield
Mary Starr - bp by Eld. Campbell
Varnum Crandall - bp Eld. Campbell
Bowland Burdick -   "   "   "
Martin Eldras -   "   "   "
Elisha Stillman - fr Scott
Prudence Stillman w/o Elisha
Prudence Stillman d/o Elisha
Thankful Stillman   "   "
Lorenzo Ayars - fr Shiloh, NJ
Jeremiah Coon - bp by Eld. Campbell
Isabella Burns - bp Mar 1838
Betsey Starr - formerly bp Eld. Matthew Stillman;
          received on Christian experience
John R. Butts - fr Otselic Feb 6, 1842
Lorana   " -   "   "   "   "
James C. Butts - fr Otselic Feb 6, 1842
Eld. James Bailey - fr 2nd Brookfield
Tacy Bailey - fr Scott

William Crandall - fr Lincklaen
Leonard Coon - bp May 29, 1842
Orson C. Coon - bp " " "
Melissa Coon - bp " " "
Dwight Stillman - bp May 29, 1842
Clarinda Miller - " " " "
D. Deloss Wells - " " " "
Miranda Cardner - " " " "
Wid. Betsey Stillman
M. Wells Crumb
Dea. Millard Wilcox - fr Scott 1842
Sybil Wilcox - " " "
Nancy " - " " "
Auredice Clark - fr 2nd Brookfield
Giles M. (illegible) - fr Lincklaen
Phebe Langworthy - fr 1st Brookfield
William B. Downer - ad Jan 1843
Hannah Downer - ad Jan 1843
John D. " - ad Mar 1843
Sarah L. " w/o John D.; ad
Hannah Wells w/o M.S. Wells; fr the M.E. Church
Maria S. Wells w/o J. B. Wells of Schenectady
Catharine C. Stillman - bp; d. Jan 1846
Fanny Wells - bp; d. Dec 9, 1843
Esther M. Crandall - bp
Mary Jane Allen - bp
Clark Bailey - bp
Sheppard Titsworth - bp
Dennis F. Coon - bp
Mary E. Crumb - bp
Alexander C. Crumb - bp
Benjamin Crumb
Ethan P Clark - fr Brookfield Nov 3, 1845
Sarah E. Drache
Lauren H. Babcock - ad Dec 13, 1846
Lucy Ann Babcock " " " "
John G. Colegrove
Ann Eliza Coon - fr 3rd Brookfield
Eld. James R. Irish - fr 1st Alfred Mar 1846
Charlotte Irish - " " " "
Mary Starr Maxson - bp Mar 1846
Jane Achley - bp Mar 1846
Levantia Burdick - bp Mar 1846
Thomas Maxson - fr 1st Baptist Church Apr 1846
Corydon B. Burdick - fr Lincklaen
Henry C. Babcock - fr 2nd Brookfield
Temperance Babcock - fr Brookfield
Welcome E. Babcock - fr 2nd Brookfield
Gusdon Evans - fr 1st Alfred
Samantha Crandall - fr 2nd Brookfield
H. Jerome Crandall - bp Apr 15, 1848
Robert Langworthy
Eliza Langworthy
Charles Langworthy

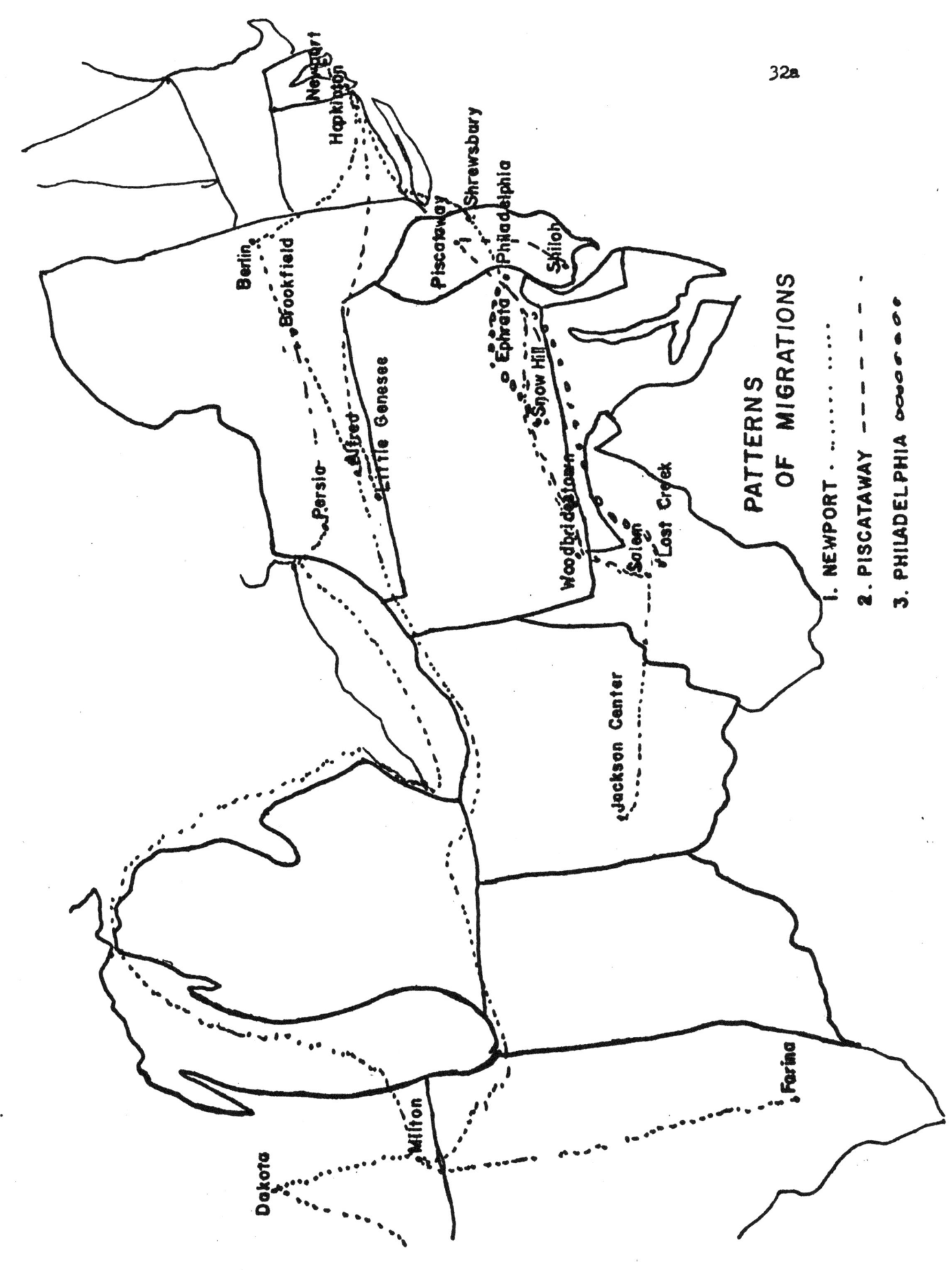

A. Judson Mills - bp Apr 22, 1848
Alfred M. Mills - bp "   "   "
Helen Lucinda Maxson
Jane Goodwin - bp Apr 22, 1848
Abigail Stillman - bp Apr, 1848
Susan Stillman - bp May 6, 1848
Antres Might - bp July 1848
Rebecca Platts - bp Nov 25, 1848
Hannah West - bp Nov 25, 1848
Jane Burdick - bp Nov 1848
Elston M. Dunn - bp July 24, 1849
Phidelio B. Gillette - bp July 24, 1849
Ira J. Ordway - bp July 24, 1849
Joseph Titsworth - bp July 24, 1849
Juliaette Worth - bp Mar 10, 1849
Phebe Ann Wilcox - bp Mar 17, 1849
Mary Starr Wilcox - bp Mar 17, 1849
Mary Livonia Burdick - bp Mar 17, 1849
Charles A. Burdick - fr Lincklaen
Edward D. Spicer - 2nd Hopkinton
Mary Lee Burdick - bp May 11, 1850
Emeline Burch - bp May 11, 1850
Hannah   "   - bp May 11, 1850
Edward Carnes - fr Scott
Mary Jane Clarke - fr 1st Hopkinton
Indus G. Cardner - bp Dec. 7, 1850
Cornelia Coon - bp Dec 7, 1850
Abby Coon - bp Dec 7, 1850
Adolph Rosen (illegible) - bp Sep 21, 1850
Adelaide Evans - bp Sep 21, 1850
Mary Maria Coon - bp Apr 26, 1850
Calista E. Peasley - bp May 30, 1851
Corydon E. Burdick - bp May 30, 1851
Hannah E. Crandall - Plainfield, NJ; bp Oct 31, 1851
Josephine Wilcox - 1st Brookfield Nov. 23, 1851
Ladurna P. Nichols - bp Jan 17, 1852
L. Adelia Nichols - bp Jan 17, 1852
J. Jerome   "   - bp Jan 17, 1852
Maria Norton - bp Jan 17, 1852
Eliza Spicer - fr 2nd Hopkinton
Harriet E. Brown - bp Mar 31, 1852
Eliza Ann Clarke - bp Mar 31, 1852
Edwin C. Williams - bp Mar 31, 1852
Arminda R. Wells - bp Arr 26, 1852
Mrs. William Crandall - bp June 5, 1852
Jane L. Crumb - bp June 5, 1852
Diadama   "   - bp June 5, 1852
Eliza Muncy - bp June 5, 1852
Margaret Quigly - bp Oct 2, 1852
Orlando Holcomb - fr Friendship
Aseneth   "   "
Elias Rogers - fr Otselic; bp Mar 1855
Content "   - fr Otselic; bp Mar 1855
James C. Rogers - Waterford CN

Clarinda Rogers w/o James C.
Sarah Ann Coon - fr Lincklaen
J.H.S. Jones - fr 1st Alfred; bp Sep 3, 1853
Sarah E. Jones " " " " " " "
Lucy Coon - fr 1st Brookfield Nov 5, 1853
Stephen B. Cardner - Truxton Nov 26, 1853
Eliza Cardner - bp in Manling
Robert Stillman - fr Lincklaen
Susan Stillman - fr Lincklaen
Mrs. Cornelia Burdick - bp Sep 1854
Ellen L. Peck - fr 1st Hopkinton
Dwight Crumb - bp Jan 6, 1855
Annie P. Crandall - fr Lincklaen
Alhanzer O. Wells - bp Mar 10, 1855
Jonathan H. Babcock- " " " "
Alburtus Clark -   " " " "
J. Bryon Whitford -   " " " "
Morell Coon -   " " " "
Marian Velpen -   " " " "
Mary J. Coon -   " " " "
Alida Muncy -   " " " "
Maria Dye -   " " " "
Emmar Burdick -   bp Mar 17, 1855
Jan. P. Wilcox -   " " " "
Sarah Langworthy -   " " " "
Leroy Maine -   " " " "
Gina   "   -   " " " "
Joel Philip -   " " " "
Franklin P. Maxson -   " " " "
Niles A. Burdick -   " " " "
Omageme Wells -   bp Mar 17, 1855
S. Cornelia Wells   " " " "
Cornelia Burdick
Livonia Langworthy - bp Mar 17, 1853
Josephine Crandall -   " " " "
Caroline S. Green -   " " " "
Elizabeth E. Burdick - " " " "
Andrew Muncy -   " Mar 2, 1855
Kenyon A. Muncy -   " " " "
FRanklin S. Wells -   " " 31, "
Welcome E. Stillman - " " " "
Julia Griffin   -   " " " "
Samuel Crumb   -   " " " "
Amy E. Irish   " " " "
Adonejah Muncy -   bp Apr 2, 1855
Carherine "   -   " " " "
Phelema Wilcox -   " " " "
Mrs. Clark Munson - fr Preston
Isaac Philips
Mary   "
Steserret C. Stillman - bp May 5, 1855
Lrander House - May 5, 1855
Mary M. Peabody - fr M.E. Church of this place
Esther North - ad June 9, 1855

Julia Stillman - bp June 16, 1855
Elizabeth Sheppey - bp June 16, 1855
Tacy Burdick - fr 2nd Brookfield
Hannah Langworthy - fr 2nd Brookfield
Eld. Thomas Fisher - fr 1st Day Baptist Church   June 1, 1856
Grace Fisher w/o Thomas - see above
Angeline Isally - fr Albion, WI
Asher M. Knapp - fr Lincklaen
Bailey Crandall - fr 1st Day Baptist Church   June 1857
Eld. J. P. Hunting - Scott Mar 13, 1858
Jennet A. Hunting - 1st Day Baptist Church of Homer
Elizabeth Coon - previously baptized
Delina Spaulding - bp Nov 28, 1857
Mrs. Thankful Coon - M.E. Church
Kenyon W. Burdick - bp Mar 4, 1859
Lorenzo Burdick - bp Mar 4, 1859
Olive Burdick w/o K. W.
Myron W. Coon - bp Mar 12, 1859
Allen Ellis -   " " " "
Mary Ellis -   " " " "
Antoinette Bentley - bp Mar 12, 1859
George Stearns - Apr 9, 1859
Wid. Hannah Burdick - ad on Christian character
Eld. J. R. Irish - reunited Sep 1859
Charlotte   "   -   "   "   "
Amy E. Irish -   "   "   "
Arsemus Stillman - bp Feb 18, 1860
Mary Jane Stillman - bp Feb 18, 1860
Asenath Burdick - fr 2nd Brookfield
Calvin B. Crandall - ad Feb 26, 1861
Charlotte J. Irish - ad Feb 26, 1861
Emily S. Burdick -   ad "   "   "
E. Jenette Spencer - ad "   "   "
Merthine Crandall -   ad "   "   "
George E. Tomlinson - Shiloh NJ Mar 1861
Amanda P.   "   - New Market NJ
Kate North - ad Apr 1861
Elizabeth Muncy - ad Apr 1861
Agnes Fox - ad Apr 1861
Arza Coon - fr 1st Alfred
Ann Eliza Coon - fr 1st Alfred
Arlouine   "   - fr 1st Alfred
George J. Crandall - fr 2nd Brookfield
Niles D. Johnson - fr Lincklaen
Henry Newton - ad Mar 22, 1862
Lucy Wilcox - ad Mar 22, 1862
Charles H. Maxson -ad Jan 31, 1863
Sena Ann Maxson - ad Jan 31, 1863
Alzeline Holcomb - ad by laying on of hands
Armelia Holcomb - ad by Christian experience   Feb 14, 1863
Mark Sheppard
DeEtta Newton - fr 2nd Brookfield
Sally Burdick - united a long time before this but for some
                neglect her name did not get on this book

Nathan Wright
Lucy M. Wright
Bradford C. Coon - fr Cuyler Hill
Alzina Coon - ad May 9, 1864
Emma Seley - bp May 9, 1864
Susan Coon - bp May 9, 1864
Isabella C. Coon - bp May 9, 1864
Charles B. Maxson - bp May 9, 1864
Henry D. Maxson - bp May 9, 1864
William S. Burdick - bp May 9, 1864
Elizabeth M. Coon - bp May 14, 1864
S. Maria Stillman - bp May 14, 1864
Amelia Burdick - bp May 14, 1864
Alanson Green - bp May 28, 1864
Thomas F. Marble - bp May 28, 1864
Sarah A. Burdick - bp May 28, 1864
Deborah Tripp - bp July 9, 1864
Mary L. Wells - bp Aug 9, 1864
Albert Whitford - fr Milton WI
Chloe " - fr Milton WI
Frank H. Babcock
Delop W. Crandall - bp May 5, 1886
Eli S. Brand - bp May 5, 1886
Charles M. Davis - bp May 5, 1886
Anna Curtis
Henry C. Coon - fr Lincklaen Feb 2, 1868
E. S. Colegrove - fr Cuyler Hill
Sally B. " - fr Cuyler Hill
Mary E. Crumb
Eld. Thomas Fisher - ad May 1, 1868
Grace Fisher - ad May 1, 1868
Mrs. E. Burdick - bp May 1, 1869
Emegene Burdick - " " " "
Edgar L. Burdick -" " " "
Edgar L. Burdick -" " " "
Maria Clark - " " " "
Jurcia O. Wells - " " " "
Freddie J. " - " " " "
Lucy Burdick - fr Lincklaen May 29, 1869
Almeda B. Langworthy - fr Lincklaen May 29, 1869
Eld. Joshua Clarke - fr Albion WI Jan 1, 1870
Esther Clarke - fr Albion Wi Apr 9, 1878
Ella F. Clarke - fr Albion WI Apr 9, 1878
Mrs. Jane Coon - ad Jan 22, 1870
Mary Sent - bp Mar 5, 1870
Libbie Coon - bp Mar 5, 1870
Arthur S. Crumb - Mar 5, 1870
Abby Coon - bp Mar 5, 1870
Harlan Hakes - Mar 5, 1870
Susie Coon - fr Adams Center
Holly M. Maxson - ad Christian experience Mar 26, 1870
Charles K. Burdick - bp 1870
Henry Green - bp
Mrs. K. V. Muncy - bp

Sylvanus Burdick - fr Lincklaen
Rosetta Burdick - fr Lincklaen
Alonza B. Langworthy - bp Mar 25, 1871
Ada Wells - bp Mar 25, 1871
Mrs. H. Burdick - bp Mar 25, 1871
Mrs. L.L. (Jennie M.) Davis - bp Mar 25, 1871
Eugene Coon - bp Apr 15, 1871
Phineas A. Burdick - fr Adams May 13, 1871
Jenny Cone - ad May 13, 1871
William M. Coon - bp 1872
Elizabeth Coon w/o William M.; bp 1872
Jerry Coon - bp 1872
Anelren Crumb - bp 1872
Mrs. Anelren Crumb - bp 1872
Celinda Rogers - fr Lincklaen Feb 1, 1878
Samuel Justice - fr Lincklaen May 17, 1873
Phineas C. Burdick - fr Cuyler Hill
Annis Burdick - fr Cuyler Hill
Mary Stone - fr 1st Genesee
Whitman Wilcox - fr Otselic Apr 1855
Phebe   " - fr Otselic Apr 1855
Sarah Jane Coon w/o M.W. Coon; ad
Jessvorie Crumb w/o Arthur; ad
Esther Dye - fr Lincklaen Apr 31, 1874
  " A. Dye - fr Lincklaen Apr 31, 1874
Minerva Babcock -bp
Eva Crop
Henry Crop
Emily Marble
Julia I. Marble - bp 1874
  Alice   "   - "   "
Charles Coon -   bp 1874
Libbie J. Coon - "   "
Elwin D. Coon - "   "
Lorne   "   - "   "
Calista M. Coon - "   "
Martin Marble - "   "
Henry H.   "   - "   "
Carrie E. Dye - "   "
Anzenette Burdick-" "
(illegible) Crop- " "
Joseph Parslow - "   "
Nancy   "   - "   "

De Ruyter, NY SDB Church Membership List
1815-1874
CRR 1967.10.7 vault   IMS:1993

List of Church Members as Revised by Committee
Appointed Apr 1892

p. 450
Dea. Jason B. Wells - bp Jun 1831; d. Jun 1836
Cornelia P. Maxson Wells - 1837; d. Jan 1898
Aetemus Coon - d . Jul 11, 1902
Thankful Coon - d. 1893
Arvilla Coon - d. 1892
J. Clark Crandall - d. Dec 4, 1914
Barton G. Stillman - d. Mar 1904
Sophronia H. Stillman - d. Mar 6, 1900
Leonard Coon - moved to Nile NY; dis Aug 13, 1892
Sarah Ann Coon - see above entry
Dennis T. Coon   - deceased
Eliza M. Coon   - deceased
Lucy A. Babcock - d. Oct 31, 1900
Mary J. Clark - d. Jun 1904
Dr. Silas S. Clark - d. May 6, 1900
Lucy Moniak Clark - d. Jul 10, 1925
Jennie L. Clark - d. Nov 19, 1922
Laderna P. Nichols - d. Mar 17, 1905
Marcilia N. Nichols - d. Apr 23, 1915
Henry C. Coon - d. Nov 24, 1902
N. Maria Coon - d. Apr 12, 1905
Elias Rogers - d. 1893
Giles D. Johnson - ad 1860; d. 1913
Helen   "   - ad 1887; d. 1906
Amy E. Irish Place - exc May 11, 1895
Philuna Wilcox Parkhurst - exc May 25, 1901
Angeline Page Cottrell
Delina Wilcox
Aseneth Burdick - d. Jul 9, 1900
Celia A. Burdick
Nellie Burdick
Myron W. Coon - exc. Jun 1898
Sarah Jane Coon - exc Apr 8, 1894

p. 452
Elizabeth M. Hays - d. 1919
Minnie Hays
Julia A. Crandall - ad 834
Antris G. Coon - d. Feb 14, 1915
Jane C. B. Armstrong - suspeneded Aug 1, 1909
Phebe A. V. Davis - 1896
Jane L. Crumb
Alcanza O. Wells - dis Apr 7, 1895
J. Leroy Maine - d. no date
Irena   "   _ d. 1896
Franklin Maxson - exc Aug 7, 1892
Mary Phillips - d. Sep 10, 1906
Alzina P. Coon - exc Jun 1898
Mary L. W. Ames

Charles M. Davis - exc May 11, 1895
Sally B. Colegrove - d. Jan 1898
Arthur S. Crumb - d. July 10, 1914
Rosa Crumb (Maxson) - d. Jan 4, 1923
Lucy Burdick w/o H.W. Burdick - d. 1894
Jane P. Davis - exc May 25, 1901
William M. Coon - d. 1895
Elizabeth Coon - d. June 1915
Andrew J. Crumb - d. Aug.18, 1900
Huldah Crumb - d. 1901
Nancy Stone - dis to Little Genesee Aug 13, 1892
Esther A. Dye
Dea. Charles M. Coon - dis to 1st Alfred Mar 1913; joined Apr 4, 1914
Clara Ellis Coon - see above entry
Libbie J. Coon Campbell - dis to 1st Alfred May 12, 1906
Lova Coon Stillman - dis Aug 113, 1892
Calista M. Coon Holmes - exc 1913
Martin Marble
Annis J. Burdick - d. Dec 5,1900
Georgianna Crofs (Wilmot) - d. 1910; dis Syracuse Aug 1, 1909
Joseph Parslow

p. 454
Nancy Parslow - dis to Syracuse Jan 18, 1909
Mary Ving - d. Dec 20, 1893
William Stirling - exc May 25, 1901
Nettie Coon Stirling - d. Apr 14, 1900
Allice Phillips Ellis - exc 1898
Pineas M. Stillman - exc 1898
Edna Maine Stillman - exc 1898
Celia Stillman Cossum - d. Dec. 8, 1895
George A. Stillman - dis to Nile NY Feb 5, 1905
Cora S. Stillman - see above
Lucy Muncy Phillips - d. Mar 20, 1915
Roswell T. Coon - d. May 1915
Effie Coon Crandall - d. Oct 31, 1900
Julia A. Lawton (?) - suspended Aug 1, 1909
Harriet Cross - d. 1890
Martha R. Cross w/o Hiram; d. no date
Henry W. Phillips
Amanda Jashie Phillips
Frank Phillips - d. May 18, 1938
Walter A. Phollips - d. May 24, 1926
Elmer Cross (?) - exc June 1878
Emma A. Marble (not Wells)
Dea. Avery C. Stillman - d. 1893
George T. Stillman
Neltie Burdick Stillman
Nina Stillman Teidell
Leona Stillman Kinney
George Cross (Syracuse) - exc June 1898
Orville L. Stillman - exc Apr 8,1894
Barney D. Crandall - d. Feb 17, 1925
Lizzie Holmes Crandall

Williston Crumb - exc June 1898
Dea. Charles J. York
Elcy Irish York
Ettie Burdick

p. 456
Joseph L. Burdick - d. 1897
B. Frank Burdick - exc 1905
George Johnson - exc Aug 7, 1892
George J. Burdick - exc June 1898
Mary Stillman Ringe - exc June 1898
Dea. J. H. Babcock - d. Mar 22, 1900
Irwin H. Babcock
Grace Babcock Cary - exc May 25, 1901
Martha Ann Marble - suspended Aug 1, 1909
Polly Stirling - d. Oct 21, 1899
Mrs. Harry Cross - exc. June 1898
Mary Seaman (?) - d. no date
Emma Crumb - exc 1901
Auvilla Marshall - d. 1899
Minnie Coon Rolles - exc 1913
Flora B. Crumb Palmer
Lora Crumb (Austin) - exc Aug 1, 1919
Frank D. Allen - dis to Scott Oct 1894
Maria Allen - see above
Horace Wells - d. 1896
Mary E. Crumb - d. 1914
Alvah B. Stewart - exc Aug 1, 1892
Mary Stewart - exc 1915
Mrs. Lyman Maxson - d. no date
Rev. L. R. Swinney - d. Mar 22, 1905
Sue M. Swinney - d. 1906
Maggie E. Swinney - exc. Aug 1, 1909
Samuel R. Stillman - d. 1897
Sarah Stillman - d. 1907
Bertha Payne Neary - exc. Apr 7, 1895
L. Bennie Burdick
Kate Phinney Benjamin - exc. May 11, 1895
F. Pearl York Babcock Gardiner
Mrs. Frank Brodinck - dis to Syracuse Jan 1, 1909
Gertie Case Smith

p. 458
Harry Case - dis to 1st Alfred Mar 8, 1900
Mwlvina West - d. 1898
Zaccheus T. Burdick - d. Jan 30, 1901
George W. Burdick
Eleanor Clark Burdick
John Greene
Mary Wilcox Locke - d. Jan 30, 1901
Eliza Wilcox Bowman
Mrs. Ida Coon - ad Nov 18, 1893; d. Jan 30, 1901
Celia Rogers Way - Nov 18, 1893; d. Aug 11, 1895
Harry Crandall - ad Aug 1893; exc June 1898

Allie Burdick (Cooler) - ad Aug 1893; d. Dec 26, 1914
Minnie Bailey Crandall - ad Aug 1893; exc. 1898
Jerry D. Coon - restored Mar 24, 1894; dis Mar 24, 1894
Mrs. Alice Annas -   Sep 1994
Miss Bertha "   -   "   "
Neil Annas   -   "   "
Mrs. Hannah Crandall-"   "   ; d. Nov 22, 1899
W. R. Philips -   "   "   ; d. no date
Mrs. W. R. Phillips- "   "   ; d. no date
John B. Swinney   "   "   ; exc 1908
Ladue Nichols   "   "   ; exc 1913
Mrs. Leurtus Palmer "   "   ; d. Feb. 27, 1925; exc 1876
Mr. Ingham   "   "   ; exc Jun 1998
Mrs. Alzina Kemp   "   "   ; d. 1898
Mrs. Ella Wilcox Annes - ad Oct 1, 1993
Frank Remington - ad Sep 1894; d. 1914
Mrs. Frank Remington "   "   ; d. Feb 11, 1915
Grant Burdick - ad   "   "   ; dis Feb 13, 1909 to West Edmeston
Mrs. Grant Burdick - "   "   ; d. 1903
Godfrey C. Mules -   "   "   ; d. 1903
Mrs. "   "   -   "   "   ; d. Feb 1916
Orin Henry -   "   "   ; d. 1910
Mrs. Orin Henry -   "   "
Eugene   "   - "   "   ; exc 1913

p. 460
Rev. L. M. Cottrell - Nov 1894; dis to Otselic 1897, restored June 1906
Ettie Phillips Weaver - exc Aug 1, 1907
Della Nichols Crumb - ad May 4, 1895
Hermon Cross June - ad 1896; dis to Syracuse Jan 1, 1909
Clara Brandt Cross w/o Hermon - see above entry
Nora Smith Burchek - ad Jun 1896
Mabel Babcock Parslow - ad Jun 17, 1896; d.Jun 17, 1912
          dis to Syracuse Jan 18, 1909
Merton Parslow - ad Jun 27, 1897   dis to Syracuse Jan 18, 1909
Mary   "   - see above
Maud Parslow Wilcox - see above entry
Frank Brodrick - ad Jun 27, 1897 Pomping Hill;dis to Alfred Feb 13, 1904
Jennie   "   - Jun 27, 1897 Pomping Hill; dis to Syracuse Jan 1, 1909
Mrs. Clarrissa Marble Smith - ad Jun 1898; d. no date
Muriel Smith d/o Clarrissa - ad Jun 1898; exc 1913
Rena Smith Jones d/o Clarrissa
Alfred Coon - ad on statement Apr 1, 1899; exc 1913
Aaron Coon - ad on statement May 6, 1899; d. no date
Willie Allen - ad May 6, 1899; dis to Alfred
John   "   - see above entry
Daisy Mules Nichols - bp May 13, 1899; dis Syracuse Jan 18, 1909
Leila Mules Coon - bp May 13, 1899; exc 1913
Robbie Mules - bp May 13, 1899; exc Aug 1, 1909
Leillan Stillman Burdick - bp Aug 1, 1909; d. no date
Rosa Henry Castles - bp Aug 1, 1909; exc 1913
Ethel Phillips Blakeman - bp Aug 1, 1909; d. no date
Leucian Wells - bp Aug 1, 1927; d. no date
Jennie S. Wells - see above entry

Robert E. Sweeney - ad May 27, 1899
Julia Wright Frink - ad Jul 7, 1900; d. no date
Millie Coon - ad Jul 7, 1900; exc 1913
Mrs. Martin Marble - ad Aug 18, 1900; d. no date
Miss Maude   "   - ad Aug 18, 1900; d. no date
Mr. H. M. Doran   - ad Aug 18, 1900; d. 1902

p. 462
Raymond Stillman - dis by letter
David Stillman - dis by letter
Raymond Burdick
Carol Burdick
Cora Coon Craft - d. June 1919
Leyman Coon - d. Oct 1966
Melvin E. Coon - dis Apr 20, 1912
Maud Coon - dis Apr 20, 1912
Ray Stillman - exc 1913
Mrs. Jesse Stillman
Julian Craft
Alice Marble
Ruby Mules
Stephen Parker - ad by letter
Mrs. Stephen Parker - ad by letter
Leon Parker - ad by letter
Mrs. Leon Parker - ad by letter
Mrs. T. R. Williams - ad by leter May 31, 1904
Mrs. Alzina Pickett - ad on statement May 31, 1904; d. Oct 8, 1914
Rev. J.J. White - on statement May 12, 1906; dis by letter
Nora Reed - bp May 26, 1906; exc Aug 1, 1909
Pauline M. Babcock - bp May 26, 1906; dis by letter
Mrs. J. H. Babcock - ad by letter Jun 30, 1906; dis by letter
Rev. L.M. Cotrell - ad by letter Jun 2, 1906; d. no date
Mrs. M. G. Frisbie - ad by letter Jul 11, 1906
M. G Frisbie - ad by Certificate Jul 11, 1906
Rev. L.A. Wing - dis by letter
Mrs. L. A. Wing - dis by letter
Loretta A. Wing - bp May 26, 1906; dis by letter
Emma E. Coon Brown - ad 1906
Isabell Smith Burdick - bp May 26, 1906
Mrs. Frank Phillips
Robert Wing
Mabel Barbour

p. 464
Maurice Lidell - bp 1912
Clesson Poole - bp 1912
Everette Poole - letter 1912; dis by letter
Ronald Babcock - bp 1912
Doris Babcock - bp 1912
George Maxson - bp 1912
Jennie Maxson - bp 1912
Archie Wing - bp 1912
Joyce Wing - bp 1912
Hubert Wing - bp 1912

Mrs. Chauncy Gasner - ad 1912; looks deliberatly erased
Mrs. Everette Poole - ad letter 1912; dis by letter
Mrs. Ann Cardner - ad letter 1912; d. no date
Mrs. John Irish - ad letter 1912
Miss Ette Crandall - bp 1912
Mr. and Mrs. Frank Kenyon - non resident; fr Nortonville KS May 9, 1914
Miss Juna Dorrvord - bp Feb 28, 1914; dis Jan 6, 1924
Mr. and Mrs. Newyon Ousler - non resident; ad Jan 23, 1915
Mrs. Arthur Crumb - ad by letter Jan 23, 1915

REVISED LIST of MEMBERSHIP   1915

RESIDENTS	DECEASED
p.455	
Lucy M. Clarke	Jan 10, 1925
Jennie "	Nov 19, 1972
Mrs. Elizabeth Hayes	1919
Minnie E. Hayes (Mrs. Robert V. Wing); dis	White Cloud MI Jul 22, 1930
Mrs. Mary Lou Ames	Nov 9, 1926
Mrs. Rosa Crumb Maxson	Jan 14, 1923
Henry W. Phillips	no date
Mrs. Amanda Justice Phillips	Aug 16, 1943
Frank Phillips	May 18, 1938
Mrs. Lida A. Phillips Coon	no date
Walter A. "	May 24, 1926
George T. Stillman	Jun 1, 1930
Mrs. Nettie Burdick Stillman	Jun 22, 1929
Mrs. Nina Stillman Lidell	no date
Ed Lidell	no date
Leona Stillman Kinney	no date
Barney D. Crandall	Feb 27, 1935
Lizzie Holmes Crandall	Oct 2, 1931
Charles J. York	May 9, 1922
Mrs. Charles J. York	Nov 19, 1923
George W. Burdick	Jan 19, 1935
Mrs. Eleanor C. Burdick	Jan 7, 1943
Mrs. Ida Coon	May 19, 1927
Mrs. Ella Wilcox Ames	Aug 18, 1931
Mrs. Orin Henry	???????????
Lucian Wells	Feb 6, 1930
Jennie L. Wells Rogers	May 25, 1932
Mrs. Julia Frink	Dec 12, 1926
Maude Marble Brown	dis Jul 12, 1927
Carrol Burdick	Aug ??, 1954
Mrs. Isabell Burdick	no date
Mrs. Cora Coon Craft	1919
Julian Craft	no date
Lyman Coon	no date
Alice Marble Stillman	dis Jul 12, 1927
p.468	DECEASED
Stephen Parker - non resident	dis July 12, 1927
Mrs. " " - " "	d. Feb 11, 1934
Leon Parker - " " 1917	resident
Mrs. " - " " "	resident
" Leurtus Palmer	Feb. 27, 1925
M.G. Frisbie	Oct 17, 1924
Mrs. M. G. Frisbie	Apr 9, 1921
Rev. L. A. Wing	dis to Boulder, CO Sep 30, 1916
Mrs. " " "	" " " " " " "
Loretta Wing	" " " " Mar 16, 1918
Robert W. Wing	dis to White Cloud, MI July 22, 1930
George Maxson	dis Jul 12, 1927
Jennie Maxson Stiener	" " " "

Richie Wing
Jorce Wing Newcomb
Mrs. John Irish   no date
Etta Crandall   Apr 12, 1942
Frank W. Kenyon   Mar 1932
Mrs. Frank "   dis Apr 13, 1940
Miss Juna Dorward Odell   dis no date
Newton Ousler
Mrs. Newton Ousler   no date
Mrs. Villis Smith   1917
Mrs. Arthur L. Crumb   Dec 20, 1933
Mrs. George Zales Alexander
Mrs. Lyman Coon
Laura Satterlee - non resident joined by letter May 14, 1916;
          dis New Market, NJ May 28, 1922
Galen Burdick - joined Sep 30, 1916; dis Lincklaen Feb. 18, 1922
Arthur Truman - non resident joined Sep 30, 1916; d. Mar 1956
Mrs. Arthur Truman - non resident   "   "   "
Mrs. Mary   "   "   "   "; d. 1919
Bessie Phillips Hinshaw -   joined "   "   "
Mildred Phillips Blowers Parker -   "   "   "   "
Miss Leola Phillips -   "   "   "   "
Rev. J. H. Hurley letter from Welton, IA Jul 7, 1917 dis Dec 2, 1918
Mrs. "   "   "   see above entry

NON RESIDENTS   DECEASED

p.470
Mrs. Delina Wilcox   Mar 20, 1922
Celia A. Burdick - dis Jul 12, 1927   1938
Nettie Burdick - dis Jul 12, 1927   Nov 27, 1946
Martin Marble   Apr 14, 1928
Etta Burdick   Jan 23, 1922
I. H. Babcock   dis Jul 12, 1927
L. Bennie Burdick   Dec 27, 1929
Pearl York Gardiner   dis Jul 12, 1927
Eliza Wilcox Bowman
Mrs. Alice Annas   May 15, 1929
Miss Bertha   "
A. Neil Annas
Mrs. Erina Coon Brown   1929
Della Nichols Crumb - resident
Nora Smith Burdick -   "
Clarissa Marble Smith   Feb 1916
Lillian Stillman Burdick   no date
Raymond C. Burdick   "   "
Mrs Martin Marble Coon
Mrs. Jesse Stillman   no date
Mrs. T.R. Williams   dis Chicago Jan 1910
Pauline M. Babcock   dis to Alfred Jul 19, 1917
Minette Clarke Babcock   dis to Alfred Jul 19, 1917
Mabel Barbour La Sure   dropped by request Oct 1931
Clesson Poole   dis to Alfred Mar 1916
E. E. Poole   "   "   "   "   "
Mrs. E.E. Poole   "   "   "   "   "
Ronald Babcock   dis July 12, 1927
Doris Babcock   dis Alfred July 19, 1917
Mrs. Harry Poole   dis Jul 12, 1927
Hubert Wing   "   "   "   "
John F. Klotzbach - ad Feb. 11, 1922
                                        dis to 2nd Brookfield May 20, 1920
Viola   "   - see above entry
J. Walter Smith   8 Hill St. Cortland
                  from Ashaway Jun 14, 1930   IMS:1993

p.472   RESIDENTS

Pastor Harold Crandall - ad fr Rockville, RI Jan 10,1920
                                        dis to New York City Oct 28, 1922
Stella B. Crandall - see above entry
Elizabeth Crandall - bp May 14, 1921; dis to New York City Oct 28, 1922
Hazel Brown Craft w/o J. M. - bp May 14, 1921
Dorothy Jones - bp May 14, 1921
Beatrice Truman Curtis - dis Brookfield 1st Baptist Church Dec 14, 1946
Margaret Ousler Stoker   see above entry
Helen Ousler Best   "   "   "
Bartley Kenyon   "   "   "
Maurice Oursler   "   "   "

Velma Lidell Defee   dis Brookfield Jul 16, 1921
Rev. John F. Randolph - ad fr Nile Dec 2, 1922;
                                        dis Milton Jct.,WI Sep 16, 1926
Emma Randolph - see above entry
Caroline   "   - "   "   "
Robert   "   - "   "   "
Mrs. E.E. Poole Gates -ad fr 1st Alfred Apr 7, 1923; d. Jun 3, 1934
Marcia Poole Fish - ad fr 1st Alfred Apr 7, 1923
Rena Smith Jones - ad Jun 1898; d. May 19, 1938
Mrs. M. G. Frisbe (2d) - ad by statement May 5, 1923; d. Nov 10, 1939
Rev. L.A. Wing - ad by statement May 26, 1923; dis Boulder May 3, 1923
Mrs. Viola Klolyback - ad fr 2nd Brookfield Feb 2, 1924
Doris E. Coon Waterbury - bp Jul 3, 1926
Phineas Cooley Burdick - bp "   "   "
Rev. John T. Babcock - ad Nov 14, 1926; dis Edinburg TX Nov 17, 1930
Arlouine Babcock - see above entry
Harold Babcock -   "   "   "
Herbert   "   -   "   "   "
Melva Babcock -   "   "   "
Lyle Babcock -   "   "   "
Isabella Remington - ad Jul 12, 1927
Harriet C. Van Horn - ad fr Piscataway NJ Dec 28, 1929
Theodore J. "   "   - "   "   "   "   "   "
Dewitt B. Coon - bp May 31, 1930
Ardale M. Coon Skaggs - bp May 31, 1930; dis Aug 5, 1935
Reginal Card -   "   "   "   "
Rosalia Card -   "   "   "   "

P.474
Arlo Burdick - bp May 31,1930
Martha D. Gates Mills - bp Jun 14, 1930
Ruth A. Gates -   "   "   "   "
Mrs. Mary Church - bp Oct 4, 1930; d. Mar 6, 1944
Harry S. Parker - by statement Jun 25, 1932
Stanley Phillips - bp Jun 25, 1932
James Burdick -   "   "   "   "
Josephine Burdick- "   "   "   "
Mariline   " - "   "   "   "
Harlow Truman -   "   "   "   "
Paul   "   -   "   "   "   "
Rex Burdick - bp Jun 24, 1933
Wendell Burdick - bp Jun 24, 1933
E. Phineas Burdick - ad by statement; d. Jul 1, 1941
Mrs. LaVern Bronson - ad by atatement;d. Aug. 9, 1934
Etta Dwight - ad by statement; d. 1935

SCOTT
Cortland Co. NY
organized 1820-c1934

NAME	SPOUSE OF	BAPTIZED or ADMITTED (If deceased, only date is given.)	FROM	DECEASED or DISMISSED
Frank D Allen		Oct 27, 1894	DeRuyter	Nov 17, 1898
John "		" 20 "		dis
Maria Allen	w/o Frank D	" 27 "		"
Willie "		" 20 "		"
Betsey Anthony		Jun 19, 1830		exc Apr 10, 1845
Charley Ayers		ad Jul 31, 1830	Salem, NJ	dis
Phoebe "		see above		

BABCOCK 1st name only given

Abel		Dec. 3, 1818		dis
Alfred B.		Apr 26, 1834		dp
Albert		Jan 26, 1878		dp
Almira	w/o Dan B.	Jul 10, 1830		
Almira	w/o Daniel Babcock	Jun 17,	DeRuyter	Mar 16, 1879
Amy	wid/o E.S.B.	Oct 11, 1818		dis
Amy	w/o Barber	Jun 23, 1832		Oct 14, 1882
Anna	w/o J. Smith	Dec 20, 1845		"
Asher M.		ad Apr 10, 1834	1st Brookfield	dis
Barbary	w/o B.B.Jr	Jun 17, 1837		Jul 8, 1846
Beriah L.		Aug 16, 1823		Aug 1852
Betsey	w/o L.B.	ad Dec 25, 1830	Truxton 1st Methodist	
Clarissa		Jan 11, 1823		dis to WI 1845
Clarissa		Jul 31, 1841		exc Nov 18, 1848
Curtes		Nov 15, 1845		exc Nov 15, 1846
Daniel		Dec 8, 1818		dis Sep 26, 1835
Daniel B.		Jun 26, 1830		dis
Daniel		ad Jun 17, 1837	DeRuyter	Jun 30, 1878
Daniel A.		Aug 21, 1844		May 27, 1877
Dennison		Nov 15, 1845		excommunicated
Edwin S.		Nov 29, 1845		dis 1857
Elsie		Jun 27, 1868		Apr 5, 1872
Emily	w/o J.B.	Nov 15, 1845		May 1, 1896
Emily	w/o Duane D. Burdick	ad Nov 1858		
Erwin		Nov 29, 1845		dis
Estelle		Jun 5, 1869		
Esther U.		Sep 4, 1841		dis
Etta		Aug 1869		Apr 30, 1903
Eunice		Apr 17 1834		dis
Eunice	w/o B.B.	Apr 23, 1842		
Experience	w/o M.B.	ad May 11, 1821	Brookfield	Jul 22, 1838
Ezra, Jr		Dec 3, 1818		Feb 12, 1878
Ezra		Mar 14, 1786	Brookfield & Stonington	Jul 16, 1844
George		Jun 30, 1832		exc Nov 26, 1836

48

BABCOOCKS continued

Name	Admitted	Place	Status
Hannah	ad Apr 14, 1821	Brookfield	Aug 1844
Hiram	Jun 5, 1830		Apr 29, 1894 84 yrs
Hiram V.	ad Dec 19, 1840	Free Will Baptist Plainfield	to Lincklaen Dec 12, 1846
Huldah w/o Kenyon	Sep 10, 1843		exc Jul 9, 1853
Jerome R.	Aug 13, 1825		Jun 1, 1867
Julia S.	Aug 1, 1830	exc Julia Skaggs	Nov 14, 1847
Jemina w/o E.P. Burdick	ad Mar 24, 1850		Mar 21, 1860
Lawson, Jr	Nov 15, 1845		exc Mar 10, 1850
Lauren H.	Jun 19, 1830		dis May 1846
Leander	Dec 6, 1845		excommunicated
Lucinda w/o E.B. Jr	Sep 8, 1816	Brookfield, Leyden MA	d. Mar 4, 1843
Lucinda	1818	Brookfield	dis
Lizzie w/o B. Townsend	Aug 1869		rejected
Loisa	Jun 10, 1831		dis
Lucy Ann w/o A.B.	Jun 16, 1823		dis
" " w/o L. H. B.	ad Dec 9, 1836	Brookfield	dis May, 1846
Lucy Elvira	May 10, 1834		dropped
Lucy L. w/o V. Brown	Aug 28, 1841		Aug 1892
Luke	ad Dec 1884	DeRuyter	Sep 14, 1878
Lydia w/o L.B.	ad May 1845	DeRuyter	dropped
Malinda	Aug 28, 1841		rj May 11, 1851
Maranda	Nov 29, 1845		Oct 1851
Marinda w/o F. Mowry	Jan 19, 1850		d. no date
Mary	ad Jun 22, 1834	1st Brookfield	dis
Nancy	Jun 26, 1830		"
Nelson	Jul 26, 1834		"
Olive w/o Wm N.B.	Feb 2, 1878		exc Mar 3, 1895
Olive	Jul 10, 1830		Mar 19, 1847
Oscar	Sep 4, 1858		dropped
Paul	Mar 18, 1786	Brookfield	Jan 24, 1840
Rouse	Jul 17, 1830		dis
Raymond	ad Jul 10, 1830		Jan 18, 1887
Ruben	Apr 11, 1834		dis
Russell	ad Mar 12, 1831		"
Saherah w/o Ezra B.	Dec 8, 1818		Apr 9, 1865
Salome	Apr 18, 1840		dis
Saviah w/o L. H.	Nov 15, 1845		Feb 20, 1913
Sophia Ann	May 10, 1834		
Teresa	Nov 15, 1845		Aug, 1859
William H.	" " "		removed
William N.	Feb 16, 1861		exc March 3, 1895
Zenira w/o E. P. Burdick	Mar 24, 1855		Mar 20, 1880

Eld. James E. N. Bachus	ad Jan 16, 1869	Watson	rem 1871
Lucy Bachus w/o J.E.N.B.	see above		
Susan Baker	Nov 11, 1837		dis Sep 2, 1848

BARBER   1st name only

Name	Date		Date 2
Alice	Jul 7, 1832		1844
Almeron	Nov 22, 1845		excommunicated
Alonzo D. C.	Jun 23, 1832		Jun 30, 1870
Alonzo D. C. 2nd	Aug 11, 1832		May 30, 1852
Alzina w/o H. Miller	Aug 1, 1874		Feb 14, 1889
Amelia	Nov 22, 1845		
Andrew S.	Feb 9, 1861		rejected
Betsey w/o Elias Green	Sep 4, 1841		1844
Bryon	Nov 29, 1845		Dec 29, 1899
Caroline w/o W.E.	May 18, 1878		
Charlotte	Nov 8, 1845		exc Mar 10, 1850
Clara	Oct 20, 1894		
Clarinda w/o B.L.B.	Mar 24, 1845		
Clark	Nov 15, 1845		exc Sep 12, 1857
Cynthia w/o S.T.W. Potter	Nov 8, 1845		Mar 1920
Diantha w/o W. S. Babcock	Jan 19, 1850		d. no date
Ennest L.	Apr 23, 1887		
Elbert	Aug 1869		rejected
Elias	Nov 18, 1845		Jan 9, 1848
Elias F.	Feb 16, 1861	restored	Feb 7, 1886
Eliza	Feb 16, 1861		Jan 1, 1910
Emily w/o C.E. Clark	Mar 31, 1855		Jun 1, 1912
Emma w/o Elias F. B.	Sep 4, 1858		Feb 28, 1915
Esther w/o M. Maxson	Aug 21, 1841		Jul 10, 1897
Esther w/o H.B.B.	Dec 20, 1845		1884
Fary	Nov 1858		killed Oct 1, 1903
Finette w/o F. C. Cobb	ad Sep 1, 1900		May 8, 1920
Frances E.	Feb 16, 1861		
Gardner	Dec 8, 1818	Alfred	1847
Gardner 2nd	Jun 23, 1832		dis
Henry	Jun 23, 1832		Feb 2, 1853
"	Dec 13, 1845		exc Jul 2, 1859
"	Jul 10, 1830		exc Dec 18, 1853
Joanne w/o J.G.B.	Jun 23, 1832		d. no date
John	Dec 8, 1878 Baptist Scott		May 4, 1860
John 3rd	Jul 7, 1832		May 8, 1860
John Jr	Nov 15, 1845		Feb 3, 1853
Lucinda	Apr 17, 1834		d. no date
Lucretia wid /o H.B.	May 10, 1834		Aug 17, 1850
Lucy Ann	Mar 1, 1861		Mar 31, 1862
Lydia w/o Andrew Babcock	Sep 4, 1841		Apr 4, 1908
Marcella	Sep 1, 1900 M.E. Church		
Marietta w/o B.S.B.	Jun 23, 1832	(Burdick)	Mar 7, 1875
Mary Ann w/o H.B.	Sep 10, 1843		Mar 7, 1853
Matilda w/o L. Green	Nov 15, 1845		d. no date
Nancy w/o M. Frink	Sep 4, 1841		Mar 24, 1904
Nettie	Sep 8, 1900		
Olivia L. w/o C. N. Knapp	Mar 24, 1855		exc Sep 5, 1861
Orrila w/o P.G.B.	Feb 16, 1861		dropped
Perry G.	Feb 16, 1861		dropped

BARBER continued   1st name only

Phebe w/o A. D. C.	Jun 13, 1830		1899
Pollina w/o John B.	Dec 8, 1818	Scott Baptist	Nov 1852
Sally w/o S. F. B.	Dec 18, 1818		d. no date
Sally w/o G. B.	Apr 11, 1834		1844
Samuel G.	Jul 20, 1817		Jul 1843
Samuel	Feb 16, 1861		
Silas	Jun 23, 1832		May 1871
Susan w/o William B.	Jun 30, 1932		Feb 20, 1895
Welcome	May 18, 1878		Jul 5, 1912
William	Jun 12, 1830		exc May 12, 1850

Sarah M. Barney w/o J. B. Richardson Ap 7,'55			May 17, 1906
Lottie Beebee w/o C. Goodell Jun 5, 1869			dp 1875
Deborah Brown	ad Aug 2, 1873		Jul 24, 1874
Fitch "	Aug 6, 1825		dis
Ruth "	Jul 14, 1832		

BURDICK   1st name only

Abbie	ad Feb 9, 1907 by letter		dis
Almeda	Nov 15, 1845		Apr 17, 1896
Amanda w/o J.B. Richardson Jan 1, 1850			Jun 15, 1858
Aminda w/o Franklin B. ad Aug 8, 1874			rej 1885
Amos	Nov 29, 1845		dis
Anna	Sep 11, 1841		Aug 11, 1880
Aramanda w/o D.D.F.B.	Nov 15, 1845		Nov 14, 1857
Aurilla	Apr 11, 1834		dis
Benjamin	Sep 4, 1841		Feb 16, 1894
Betsey	Aug 4, 1832		Sep 12, 1839
Clark	ad Apr 19. 1834	Berlin	dis
Clark	ad Nov 22, 1845		gone out
Daniel	Apr 11, 1834		1847
Diana	Jun 23, 1832		Aug 7, 1858
Dolphin D.	ad Nov 24, 1845		Mar 6, 1908.
Duane D. F.	Apr 7, 1855		dropped
Edwin P.	ad Mar 24, 1855		
Elbert V.	Aug 1869		Jul 23, 1875
Elias	ad 1853	Truxton	dis 1854
Electa	Jul 3, 1830		dis
Elizabeth wid/o Jabez B.	Aug 14, 1830		d. no date
Emerson	Feb 16, 1861		Apr 17, 1872
Emma w/o F. O. B.	ad Dec 14, 1886	Utica,WI	dis
Euretta w/o Lee B.	ad Jan 18, 1850	Baptist Spafford	d. Aug 6, 1903
Fred F.	Aug 29, 1885		
Eld. F. O.	ad Dec 14, 1886	Utica, WI	dis
Ferrill	Jun 23, 1832		"
Harriet w/o E.P.B.	ad Mar 1, 1861	Methodist	April 8, 1907
Henry	ad Jul 31, 1830	Hopkinton RI	Oct 25, 1868

BURDICK continued

Henry Lee		Jul 17, 1830	1890
Jemina w/o H. Burdick		Apr 26, 1834	Jun 22, 1850
Jesse		Jul 17, 1830	Sep 12, 1858
Jesse 2nd		Sep 3, 1825	dis Sep 23, 1845
Joel G.		Mar 24, 1855	Nov 12, 1865
Joseph	ad	Apr 14, 1821 Brookfield	Feb 1852
Joseph T.		Jun 23, 1832	Feb 18, 1893
Judith wid/o H.B.	ad	Mar 10, 1821 Brookfield Scott	May 1838
Katharine	ad	Sep 3, 1825 Brookfield Berlin	dis Sep 23, 1845
Lilla		Aug 8, 1874	
Louisa w/o P. Knight		Apr 18, 1840	Jan 7, 1906
"		Nov 22, 1845	gone out
Lucy		Jul 23, 1825	dis
Marrilla	ad	Jan 13, 1822	"
Magaretta		Aug 11, 1832	"
May		Jun 5, 1865	
Nancy	ad	May 10, 1834 Brookfield Cozenovia	dis
Perry V.	ad	Apr 20, 1822 Hopkinton RI	dis
Perry	ad	Dec 19, 1827 " "	Mar 13, 1849
Phoebe w/o S.M.B.		Jul 14, 1832	May 10, 1878
Polly		May 11, 1822	Feb 9, 1880
Polly	ad	Apr 19, 1834 Berlin	dis
Polly w/o Clark Burdick	ad	Nov 22, 1845	gone out
Rosina w/o J. B. Whiting		Mar 24, 1855	dropped
Roxanna w/o E.H.P. Potter		July 7, 1832	Apr 17, 1900
Russel		Jun 23, 1832	exc Jul 13, 1845
Sally		Dec 28, 1818	Apr 26, 1876
Sally		Jun 26, 1830	1843
Survilla w/o F.S. Hazard		Nov 15, 1845	Jun 3, 1906
Tacy	ad	Dec 18, 1827 Hopkinton RI	Jul 25, 1852
Temperance	ad	Apr 20, 1822 "	dis
Thompson		Aug 7, 1830	"
Willit	ad	Jan 13, 1822	"
Horace Burr		Jul 14, 1832	exc May 14, 1837
Ruhamen " w/o S.B.	ad	July 31, 1830 Berlim Scott	dis
Anna Campbell w/o Eld. Orson	ad	Dec 9, 1836	"
Eld. Orson Campbell	ad	Dec 9, 1836	1839
Edwin Carnes		Nov 29, 1845	dis Mar 28, 1850
Edward "	ad	Dec 27, 1851 DeRuyter	exc Jul 2, 1854
Ann T. Chapman		Feb 23, 1861	dp
Orville Churchill	ad	Jul 30, 1910 by letter	

CLARK 1st name only

Albert	Feb 16, 1878	Mar 9, 1896
Alvah	Apr 18, 1895	dis
Amanda w/o Dea. C. Clark ad	Aug 4, 1823 Hopkinton	"
Artelia w/o D.A. Clarke	Jul 31, 1841	Nov 11, 1884
Bennet	Nov 29, 1845	1909

CLark continued

Name	Date	Place	Status
Caroline w/o Corydon C.	ad Dec 27, 1855	1st Day Baptist	dp
Charles A.	Aug 7, 1875		d. no date
Charles E.	Jan 19, 1850		1876
Dea Charles	ad Aug 4, 1823	Hopkinton	dis
Chauncey	Feb 23, 1861		Sep 25, 1864
Clayton	Oct 27, 1894		
Corydon	Nov 29, 1845		dropped
Delos	Dec 6, 1845		exc Nov 18, 1848
Elizabeth J.	Feb 9, 1878		
Ella	Jun 5, 1869		dis Nov 1886
Emily	Apr 26, 1834		exc 1855
Emmy w/o W. Edget	Nov 29, 1845		d. no date
Eunice w/o J.B.Clark	Jun 7, 1856		dropped
George S.	Feb 9, 1878		rej Jul 12, 1885
George	Dec 6, 1863		Apr 4, 1883
Gracie	Jan 26, 1878		dis Aug 1889
Job	Jul 17, 1830		d. no date
Katie	Jan 19, 1878		
Leila	Aug 8, 1874		Jul 13, 1875
Lois w/o wid P.S.C.	ad Jan 9, 1850		Sep 16, 1894
Maria	May 17, 1834		exc Sep 13, 1835
Martha w/o O. Potter	Feb 6, 1858		May 3, 1914
Martha wid	Dec 8, 1818		dis
Mary	ad May 9, 1830	Brookfield	Jan 24, 1887
Minette w/o Babcock	Mar 20, 1886		dis
Myra w/o Gould	Apr 18, 1885		dis Apr 7, 1910
Randolph	Aug 1869		rej
Ray P.	Jun 3, 1854		"
Roscoe A.	Mar 20, 1886	joined Alfred 1892	
Theresa w/o S.C. Stillman	Jun 3, 1854		standing removed
Thomas	ad Jun 12, 1930		
William H.	Feb 16, 1861		1871
Wright	Jun 17, 1837		dis
Calvin Cobb	Jul 25, 1874		
Eld Amos W. Coon	ad Feb 10, 1855	Albion WI	removed standing
Annie Coon w/o A.W.C.	ad May 26, 1872	Lincklaen	dis Mar 18, 1879
Eunice "	see above		
Josephine Coon	see above		
Louisa w/o A.W.C.	Feb 14, 1857	First Day Baptist	d. no date
Martha w/o A.W.C.	ad Feb 10, 1855	Albion Wi	Nov 10, 1856
Rena Coon	Jul 11, 1874		dis Mar 18, 1879
Daniel Cottrell	May 9, 1821		Feb 19, 1835
" W. "	Jan 19, 1850		dp
Eunice "	ad Jul 3, 1830	Methodist	dis
John B. "	ad " " "	"	"
Meribe wid/o D.E.	ad May 17, 1824	Hopkinton	Feb 20, 1848
Peleg Cottrell	Aug 14, 1841		Mar 1, 1872
Sally " w/o Jeramiah	Mar 6, 1820	DeRuyter	exc Dec 17, 1835

William "	Jun 23, 1832	" Nov 26, 1836
Elizabeth Ann Crandall	May 11, 1822	dis
Martha Crandall	Jun 23, 1832	"
Olive Crandall	Jun 17, 1837	"
Edmund Crosley	Dec 20, 1845	exc Mar 7, 1858
James "	ad Jun 10, 1831 Alfred	Aug 20, 1890
Maryanne " w/o C. Sweet	Nov 29, 1845	dis
Pollina "	Aug 6, 1825	May 20, 1874
Bridget Dalton	ad Feb 19, 1848	dp
Isaac Darling	Oct 20, 1894	"
Allie Davis	Jan 26, 1878	dis Oct 1, 1878
Darius K. Davis	ad May 29, 1875 Hartsville	" " " "
Lucinda " w/o Darius K. Davis	see above	
Rev R. G. Davis	ad Jun 1906	dis 1908
Viola Davis	see above	
Betsey Dye	ad Aug 9, 1823	May 24, 1861
David P. "	Jul 10, 1830	dis
Orisa "	" " "	"
Thomas "	ad Aug 9, 1823	d. no date
Rev W. H. Ernst	ad May 9, 1903 Dodge Center MN	dis
Mrs. V. H. "	see above	
William M. Edgett	ad Nov 1858 Methodist	
Willie Edgett	Jun 5, 1869	rj
Amelia Fenton w/o J. Fenton	Oct 24, 1894	
Harmony Ferry	ad Jun 27, 1868	Apr 24, 1887
Emerson Fisk	ad Dec 27, 1913	
Maude " w/o Emerson Fiske	see above	
Cynthia Fowler w/o C.F.	Aug 13, 1825	dis

FRINK   1st name only

Almira	May 11, 1822	dis
Alzina	Sep 14, 1822	dis
Araminda	Jun 1840	dis
Betsey w/o J.B. Green	Apr 18, 1840	Dec 4, 1891
Climena	May 17, 1834	dis
Elias	Apr 11, 1834	dis
Emmeline	Nov 29, 1845	d. no date
Electa	Sep 11, 1841	dis
Esther	ad Dec 19, 1827 Brookfield	exc Apr 17, 1836
Esther	ad Nov 15, 1823 Methodist Lyden	" Mar 12, 1837
Ezekial	Jun 1840	
George	Dec 8, 1818	dis
George Jr	Dec 8, 1818	dis
Horace	Jun 1840	exc Aug 15, 1836
Joseph B.	ad Jun 1840	gone out
Lizana w/o Francis N. Hazard	Jun 5, 1869 Brookfield	exc Apr 17, 1836
Louisa	Nov 15, 1845	rj Nov 8, 1903
Mary w/o J.F.	ad Nov 15, 1845	exc Nov 10, 1851

FRINK continued

Nancy	Aug 17, 1820	d. no date
Oliver	Dec 6, 1845	dis
Prudence	Aug 28, 1841	1848
Sherman	Jun 1840	1852
Tacy, H. Babcock	Jul 14, 1832	dis
Theda	Jul 14, 1832	Jun 28, 1893

FRISBIE   1st names only

Anna	Apr 18, 1855		
Carrie w/o William	Jun 5, 1869		
Elias	Feb 9, 1861		rj
George	Jul 26, 1834		dp
George N.	ad Jul 26, 1834		exc July 11, 1852
Hannah w/o G.N.F.	ad Mar 1, 1861		Sep 2, 1898
Martha w/o Mills G.F.	ad Mar 1, 1861		Jul 3, 1869
Mary M w/o J. Schuyler	Aug 21, 1841		dis
Mills	Feb 9, 1861		exc Nov 14, 1857
Mills G.	ad Mar 1, 1861		dp
Willie	Oct 20, 1894		dp
Myrte Fuller	Apr 23, 1887		Jun 8, 1896
Henry J. Garthwait	Jun 16, 1832		dis
Nancy "	Apr 12, 1834		dis
Mary Gilbert	ad May 11, 1822		Sep 15, 1856
Dean Gould	Jun 23, 1832		rj Nov 15, 1835

GREEN 1st name only

Alvira w/o A. Clark	Sep 4, 1841		1896
Arthur	Feb 16, 1878		
Daniel A.	ad Feb 23, 1878	1st Alfred	1887
Elias	ad Dec 13, 1845		dp
Emily w/o G.S.Green	ad Oct 8, 1830	Truxton M.E.	Mar 12, 1868
George	ad Apr 18, 1840	1st Alfred	Apr 24, 1898
Harriet N. w/o H.B. Burr	Apr 16, 1834		exc May 1858
Harriet w/o G.W.G.	Nov 22, 1845		Feb 25, 1893
Eld Joel	Jul 5, 1818	M.E.-Spafford	dis
Marian V. w/o A.D. Prentice	ad Mar 24, 1855	DeRuyter	dis 1863
Nancy w/o Eld Joel Green	Jul 7, 1816	Baptist-Scott	dis
William	Jun 23, 1832		dis

Benajah Hall	Jul 28, 1832		exc Mar 12, 1837
Horace Haskal	ad Mar 10, 1855	Mc Growville	gone out
Betsey Hayes wid/wo D.C.H.	Aug 12, 1820;		exc Betsey Anthony 1840
Eunice Hayes	Sep 11, 1841		exc Jul 9, 1853
Eva Hazard	Sep 1, 1800		
Lewis Hazard	Nov 29, 1855		Mar 18, 1905
Sylvester Hazard	Aug 1869		

HUBBARD 1st name only

Name	Admitted	Status
Amy wid/o J.H.	ad Nov 10, 1827 Berlin	Dec 19, 1838
Amy, 2nd	" " " " "	Nov 12, 1868
Amy w/o J.H. Crandall, Jr	ad Nov 10, 1827 Berlin;	April 16, 1886
Anna	ad Nov 10, 1827 Berlin	dropped
Diane w/o H.C. Hubbard	ad Dec 19, 1827 Brookfield	dis
Etta	ad Aug 6, 1864	May 20, 1875
Eunice	Nov 22, 1845	Oct 23, 1857
Franklin	Jul 31, 1841	removed standing
Flora G.	Mar 24, 1855	Jan 3, 1874
Henry A.	May 1, 1830	Mar 1867
James	Nov 10, 1827 Berlin	May 12, 1855
Joseph	Nov 22, 1845	removed
Mary w/o J. Pratt	Nov 8, 1845	Jun 2, 1909
Tacy	ad Nov 10, 1827 Berlin	dis
Malinda Hull w/o Eld V. Hull	ad Jan 19, 1850	dis
Eld V. Hull	ad Jan 19, 1850	dis
Richard "	Jan 19, 1850	dis
Alzina Hunt	Oct 27, 1894	Jan 6, 1901
Lydia Hunt w/o S.H.	Dec 2, 1820	Jan 29, 1878
John P. Hunting	ad May 5, 1805 1st Day Baptist Conn.	dis Dec 3, 1857
Lucy Huntington wid	ad Nov 10, 1820	rj Sep 10, 1837
Philena " wid/o T.H.	Mar 17, 1822	dis
Eld William Jones	ad Aug 6, 1864 Plainfield NJ	rem
Mary A. Kelly	Nov 8, 1845	exc Jan 1858
Betsey Kinyon wid/o J.K.	May 5, 1821	dis
Charlotte " w/o H.K.	ad Feb 1, 1861 First Baptist	"
Eunice "		
Justus Kinyon	ad Jan 13, 1838 Methodist	
John L. "	ad Jan 13, 1837 Free Will Baptist-Niles	
	dis 1st C. Verona Jan 17, 1938	
Justus "	ad May 4, 1833 Berlin	dp
Asher Knapp	Apr 17, 1834	dp
Clarence N. Knapp	Mar 24, 1855	exc Sep 5, 1861
Oliva Knapp w/o C.N. Knapp	1908	
Philander Knight	ad Aug 6, 1864	dis Jan 22, 1882
Abel G. Lewis	Jul 7, 1832	exc Dec 23, 1843
" " "	1853	dis
Abraham H. "	Nov 29, 1845	d. no date
Datus E. "	Mar 19, 1832	dis
Katherine " w/o R.R. Lewis	ad Jan 13, 1838	exc May 13, 1849
Martha " w/o A.G. Lewis	ad 1853 2nd Brookfield	dis
Russell R "	ad Jan 13, 1838 " "	exc Jul 1849
Tacy "	Jul 17, 1832	dis
Virtue "	ad Jun 26, 1830 Truxton	Apr 27, 1838
Cyprian Marsh	ad May 12, 1838 Niles	exc May 13, 1849

MAXSON   1st name only

Name	Added	Removed
Abigail wid/o A. Bell	Aug 16, 1823	Mar 24, 1869
Adelia S. w/o W.H.M.	Mar 1, 1861 Methodist	Feb 7, 1893
Ardie	Aug 1869	Mar 14, 1873
Almira	Sep 4, 1841	exc Feb 2, 1851
Charles L.	Feb 16, 1861	d. no date
Deborah	ad Aug 4, 1832 Brookfield	1884
Delight	Aug 21, 1841	exc mar 13, 1849
Diantha	Nov 18, 1820	dis
Ellen w/o H.D.M		exc Sep 8, 1867
Elna w/o Geo. Hall	Jul 18, 1874	
Emmaline w/o Dr. G.W.M. baptized twice and joined twice: 1st Jul 18, 1874, 2nd Dec 30, 1854; d. May 19, 1855		
Franny E.	Aug 21, 1841	exc May 13, 1849
Franny wid/o Elnethen M.	ad Oct 1854 Brookfield	Apr 15, 1886
Fedelia w/o N. Hall	Jul 18, 1874	Sep 28, 1892
Florence w/o Farley	Jul 11, 1874	dp 1885
Francis	Jan 26, 1878	
George T.	ad Apr 18, 1840 3rd Brookfield	Jul 26, 1844
Henry	Aug 4, 1832	Apr 24, 1872
Hannah M.	Aug 28, 1841	exc May 1, 1851
Harriet	ad Aug 8, 1846 Baptist	gone out
Henry J.	ad Nov 1858	exc Sep 8, 1867
Ida w/o F.M.M.	ad Nov 27	
Ida w/o Orris Getman	ad Aug 1869	
Ira	ad Feb 9, 1861	Mar 1904
Jane w/o Gaylord Maxson	ad Mar 24, 1855	dis
Judith wid/o H.M.	Dec 8, 1818	"
Kate w/o J.M.	Mar 1, 1861	May 17, 1868
Lodenea w/o Amos M.	Mar 31, 1855	Feb 22, 1877
Lottie	Sep 8, 1900	
Luvern	Jul 31, 1847	Excommunicated
Minerva w/o Wilbur M.	Aug 17, 1902	
Morgan	Mar 24, 1855	Jun 21, 1894
Orlesta w/o M. Harrington	Feb 9, 1878	dp
Peter	Nov 15, 1845	gone out
Shurl D.	Nov 15, 1845	gone out May 1865
Silas	Jul 3, 1830	dis
Susan	Feb 10, 1822	dis
Welcome	ad Jun 19, 1830	dis
Wilbur H.	ad Mar 1, 1861 First Day	Mar 15, 1905

Name	Added	Removed
Addison Palmer	Nov 29, 1845	dis
Huldah " w/o Norman P.	ad Jun 24, 1848 SDB Eulysons PA; dis VI'54	
Lucy B. " w/o Proter Brown	Mar 24, 1855	dp
Norman "	ad Jun 24, 1848 SDB Eulysons PA;	Dis VI 1854
Sophia " wid/o H.P.	ad Oct 3, 1856	d. no date
Tabitha Ann Palmer w/o C.S.P.	Nov 22, 1845	" " "

Green Palmiter   ad May 12, 1838
          Freewill Baptist Plainfield NJ   dis Jul 11, 1849
Nancy Palmiter   see last entry

May Pidge w/o Will P.	Oct 20, 1894	dp
Will "	see above	
Rev J.A. Platt		dis Jun 1, 1892 to Leonardsville
Ella Pratt w/o S. J. Hazard	Jun 26, 1869	
Ethan Pray	Jan 6, 1838	dis

POTTER 1st name only

Abigail w/o E.G.P.	1811 Berlin	Jun 12, 1890
Alzina w/o Berdet Hayes	Jun 15, 1869	dis May 19, 1884
Bourden	Feb 16, 1861	May 17, 1912
Clark S.	Aug 28, 1841	Dec 2, 1868
E. H. P.	Jun 23, 1832	Jun 22, 1905
Elizabeth N. w/o H.E.J.P.	ad Dec 7, 1872 DeRuyter	Oct 4, 1913
Ezekial G.	ad Jul 18, 1820	Sep 7, 1869
Harlan E. J.	Feb 23, 1861	Oct 29, 1911
Hiram	Jun 30, 1832	dis
Julia Ann w/o Barber	Jul 24, 1830	Dec 31, 1837
Lavanche w/o B.H.P.	Jun 1, 1878	Feb 6, 1883
Leman	Aug 1869	
Mary w/o A.G.Green	ad Aug 1869	
Nellie w/o L.W.P.	Oct 20, 1894	
Rachel	Apr 26, 1834	Dec 4, 1838
Stephen T. M.	Aug 28, 1844	May 28, 1904
Winifred	Oct 20, 1894	

Davison F. Randoph	ad May 5, 1855 Preston	exc Jul 24, 1858
Susan L. Rees w/o Wm Res	Apr 7, 1855	dp

Aaron Richardson	Sep 25, 1855	rj Sep13, 1835
Experience "	ad Jan 8, 1825 Baptist IN	dis
Gersham "	ad " " "	rj Sep 13, 1835
James B. "	Mar 24, 1855	Sep 3, 1864
Joseph "	Jun 26, 1830	rj Sep 23, 1835
Milo "	Mar 24, 1855	dp
Polly "	Aug 11, 1832	rj Sep 13, 1835

Arletta E. Rogers w/o Rev B.F	Oct 27, 1894 Berlin	dis
Rev. B. F. "	see above	
Cinderella Scott w/o Rev. J.L.S.	Jul 7, 1832	dis
Lucy Ann Searls w/o C. Holmes	Nov 29 1845	d. no date

Asa Smith	ad Nov 11, 1823 Brookfield, Dighton MA	dis
Daniel "	Jul 31, 1830	exc
Isaac "	ad Mar 7, 1855	dis
James M."	Jul 10, 1830	exc Nov 13 1836
Lucinda Smith w/o A.S.	Jun 12, 1830	dis
Martha "	Jan 8, 1825	dis
J. Riley K. Smith	Apr 18, 1885	Dec 1, 1897
Shubal Smith	ad Nov 11, 1823 Brookfield, Dighton MA	dis
Josie Stanton w/o C.B.S.	Jan 26, 1878	Apr 6, 1911

STILLMAN 1st name only

Name	Date	Place	Status
Alfred	Jan 26, 1878		dis Jun 1893
Allen P.	Apr 18, 1885		
Betsey	ad Aug 2, 1883	Methodist	dis
Clark	ad Feb 3, 1822	Hopkinton	Mar 30, 1839
Elisha	ad May 17, 1824	Hopkinton	dis
Ira	ad May 9, 1830	Hopkinton	dis
Jared Jr	ad Jan 13, 1822		dis
Myra	Jun 7, 1879		died in CA
Prudence	ad May 17, 1828	Hopkinton	dis
" 2nd	see above		
S. C.	ad Mar 16, 1879	Richburg NY; dis winter 1892-1893	
Mrs. S. C.	see above		
Stennet C.	ad Aug 1859	DeRuyter	dp
Thankful	ad May 17, 1828	Hopkinton	dis

William B. St.John	ad Sep 11, 1875 Homer		
	withdrawn by his own request		Dec 1897
Andrew Sweet	Jan 19, 1850		exc Mar 14, 1852
" " Jr	Feb 16, 1861		Feb 28, 1863
Clark "	Jan 19, 1850		dis
Hannah E." w/o Stephen S.	Jan 26, 1850		d. no date
Stephen "	Jan 26, 1850		Excommunicated 1870
Mary Ann Tracey	Jul 31, 1830		dis
Antoinette Truman	ad Jun 27, 1869 Cupawago PA		dp Mar 3, 1878
Irving P. "	see above		
Huldah w/o W.G.	Jul 23, 1825		dis
Eld Job Tyler(Tyer)	Jan 10, 1824 Methodist-Marcellus		dis
Sally " " w/o Eld Tyler	May 14, 1825 Methodist		dis
Louisa Van Aire	Feb 16, 1861		dp
Angline Van Ever	Feb 20, 1861		dp
Lucy Welch w/o A. Anthony	Jun 26, 1830		exc 1840

Angeline Wells	Sep 6, 1834 Petersburg		exc May 12, 1849
Eliza " w/o E. W.	ad Sep 11, 1842 2nd Brookfield		gone out
Emily " w/o V.B.W.	Dec 30, 1837		dis Sep 2, 1848
Justus H. "	Jul 19, 1834 Brookfield-Grafton		dis
Jason "	ad June 22, 1834 Genesee		dis
Mary Jane "	Dec 20, 1845		dis Aug 2, 1848
Myrtal "	Nov 8, 1845		dis Sep 2, 1848
William B."	ad Dec 30, 1837 2nd Brookfield		dis 1848

Rev. J.J. White	ad May 1880		dis Nov 1883
Sarah "	see above		
Anson L. Whiting	Jun 23, 1832		Apr 24, 1897
Nancy " w/o A.L.W.	Jun 23, 1832		May 27, 1877
Jeremiah "	Nov 15, 1845		exc 1851
" "	Dec 20, 1845		dp
Lucelia " w/o S.A. Childs	Dec 6, 1845		1889
Mary Whiting w/o Cershoe	Apr 7, 1855		dp

Anna Willcox w/o Henry W. Jun 1838   exc May 13, 1849

Esther Wilcox w/o H.W.	ad Sep 11, 1842 SDB-RI		gone out
Fanny Willcox	Apr 17, 1832 1st Brookfield		dis
Harry "	Jun 15, 1833		dis
Josephine "	Apr 13, 1844		dis June 10, 1846
Loren "	Jul 23, 1825		exc Sep 13, 1835
Loren "	ad Sep 10, 1843	restored	gone out
Martin "	ad Jul 23, 1820 Burlington CN		dis Jun 10, 1846
Mehitable " w/o M.W.	Aug 14, 1824		" " " "
Matilda "	Jun 23, 1832		dis 1844
Sarah "	Apr 13, 1844		dis Jun 10, 1846
Sybil " w/o Villard V.	1823		dis
Willard "	Jan 4, 1825		dis
J. Lewis Wilson	Feb 16, 1878		
Anna Winchester	Oct 20, 1894		
Emma "	" " "		
Leonard Woolworth	ad Apr 18, 1840 First Alfred		dis

SCOTT NY SDB CHURCH LIST of MEMBERS
compiled by Mrs. Lisle Cottrell   B-File
IMS   1993
Original records at Cornell University   IMS:1993

LINCKLAEN
Chenango Co., New York
Sabbath School organized: 1828
Church organized: 1831-c1950

A List of Names Belonging to the Seventh Day Baptist Church
in
Lincklaen Jan 17, 1848
(If deceased, only date is given)

NAMES	DISMISSED RESIDENT DECEASED	NAMES	DISMISSED RESIDENT DECEASED
p. 1			
George Burdick	Feb 11, 1850	Vestia Burdick	
Samuel Stillman	Jun 25, 1853	Grace Stillman	May 13, 1854
Elisha Stillman	Jun 15, 1855	Flavilla Stillman	
Thomas Stillman		Benjamin H. Burdick	
Senylen D. Crandall	dis	Almeda Stillman	
Matthew Stillman	May 14, 1849	Diana M. Stillman	
Avery C. Stillman		Cyrus Cartwright	
Olive Saunders		Cornelia Burdick	dis
Salina M. Cartwright		Polly Ann Main	dis
Emily H Main	dis	Celina Austin	Mar 4, 1849
Benjamin S. Burdick		William Stillman	Jul 17, 1852
Elvira Nichols	dis	Susannah Cartwright	
Abigail Stillman		John Dye	May 18, 1855
Henry Olin	Ap 10, 1854	Emma Crandall	dis Jan 14, "
Hannah R.C. Cartwright		Celinda Olin	
Polly Coon	dis	Martha Crumb	
Lydia Champlin	dis	William E. Burdick	Aug 24,'50
Lucy Burdick	d. no date	Jonathan Crandall	dis 1855
Sanford B. Stillman		Estrus P. Nichols	dis
Lucy Olin		Daniel C. Burdick	
Maria Burdick		Emily Main	dis
Clarissa Burdick			
p.2			
Henry C. Burdick		Elinor Ann Crandall	Sep 21,'50
Jared Stillman		Clark Coon	
Betsey Coon		William G. Crandall	
David W. Wells	dis	Catherine Wells	dis
Schuyler Olin		Wait Burdick	dis
Orra Olin	Mar 18, 1850	Adelia Stillman	
Sarah Ann Stillman	dis	Briant Cartwright	dis
Abram Coon		Esther Coon	
Horace Burdick	exc Nov 11, 1849	Polly Ann Nye	exc
Julia Ann Marble		Thomas H. Burdick	
Polly D. Carpenter	dis	Willit S. Burdick	dis
Martha Burdick		Jared Maxson	d. no date
Amy Maxson	dis	Lydia Carpenter	dis
Matilda Babcock	dis	Alsada Cartwright	
Arvilla Burdick	rj	Alnora Babcock	dis
Elinor Ann Crandall	Sep 21, 1850	Mary Saunders	dis

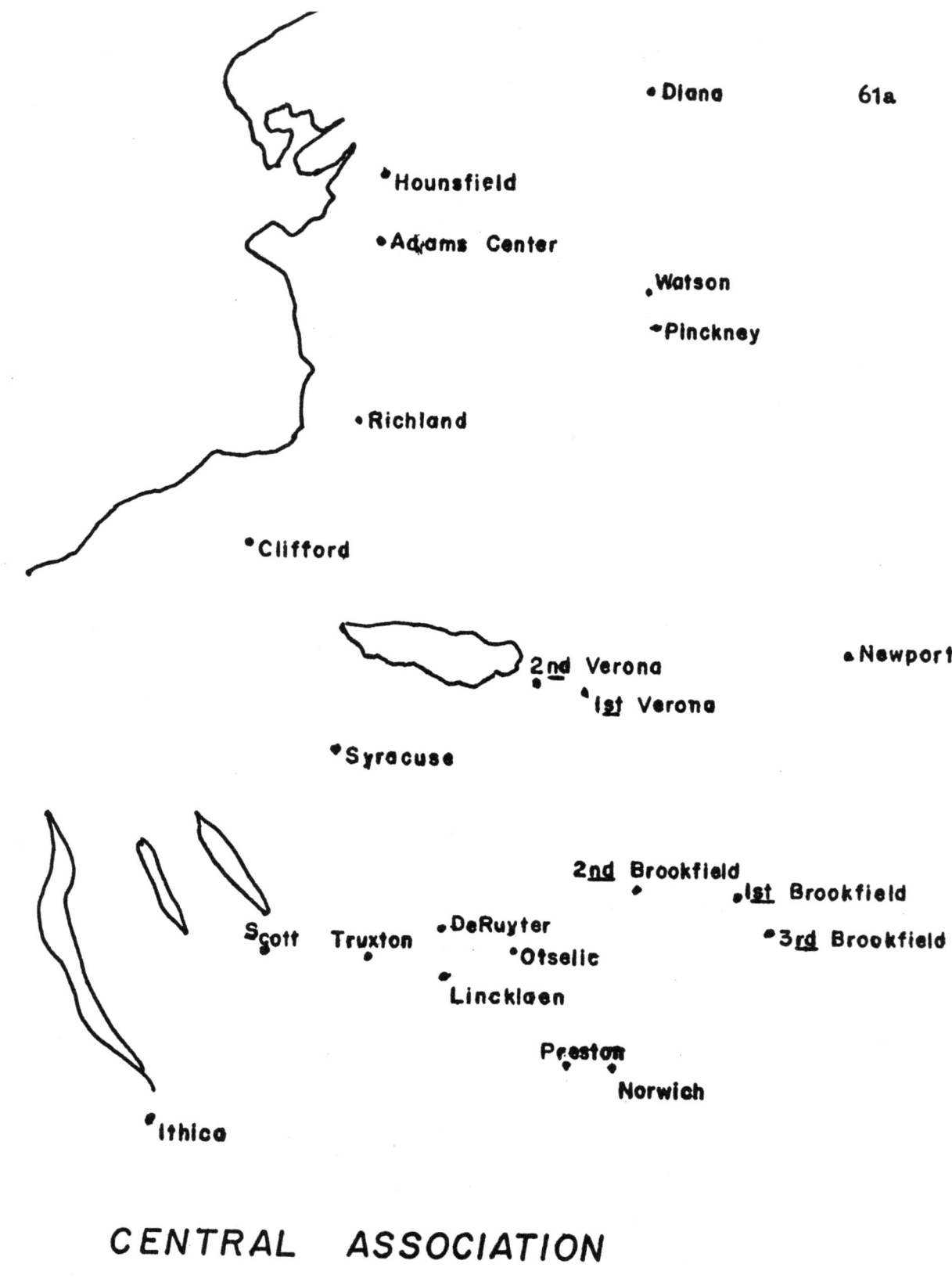

CENTRAL ASSOCIATION

Weltha A. Babcock
Thomas B. Coon   dis
Samuel R. Stillman
Maxson Stillman
Temperence L. Burdick
Susan Burdick
Minerva Coon
Lafayette Carpenter   dis
Hannah Carpenter   dis

John G. Burdick   dis
Kinyon B. Coon   dis
Adison Burdick   dis
Clarissa Burdick   dis
Polly E. Burdick
Jane Coon
Howard Stone
Stepen V. Carpenter   dis
John P. Dye   dis

p. 3
Sally A. Dye
Lovena Johnson   dis
Stephen W. Wells   dis
Lohansa Burdick
Mary Stillman
Orlando Dye
Lucy Ann Muncy   dis
Samuel Justice
Lucinda Justice
Rosetta Nicholas
Charles A. Burdick   dis
Celinda Burdick   dis
Sarah S. Stillman   dis
Robert Stillman   dis
Norman Burdick
Azuba Davis   Aug 18, 1850
Kenyon Burdick   Jr
Asa Coon   1861
Lydia Burdick
Barbary J. Ackley   Sep 1852
Alexander Campbell   dis
Jerome Hall   dis
Pluma V. Wells   dis
George Campbell   dis

Harriet Lyon
Eliphlet H. Johnson   dis
Amanda Stillman
Weltha M. Burdick   dis
Clarinda Dye
David C. Coon
Harriet Burdick
Jane Stillman
Mary Ann Stillman
Edward Burdick
Spaulding Burdick   rj
Eliza Burdick   Oct 7, 1850
Nancy C. Stillman
Spencer Burdick
Sophia Carpenter   dis
Daniel Lyon
William Coon   Apr 9, 1852
Mary Ann Coon
Lovina Burdick   dis
William F. Babcock   exc
Clarinda Campbell   dis
Emma Hall   dis
Hiram W. Babcock   dis

p. 4
Sylvanus Burdick
Polly A. Crandall   dis
Jane Burdick   dis
Juliette Crandall
Elvira Crandall   Oct 19, '50
Cornelia Olin
Martha R. Burdick
Emily Crandall dis Jan 14, '?5
Ruth Crumb   Dec 6, 1853
Orvill Stillman   1851 resident

Almina Coon   Mar 27, 1851
Susan Stillman   dis
Weedon Burdick   dis
Elizabeth Saunders   Jan 14, '55
Luanna Burdick
Martha Olin
Welcom B. Crandall   d. no date
Lebicus M. Burdick   dis 1853
Lucinda Maine

1852

Lewis Z. Burdick   1852
Charles H. Crandall   dis
Benjamin Stillman   withdrew Mar 12, 1856
Rev. Russel Z. Burdick dis   Adeline Burdick   dis

Elizabeth F. Burdick
Sarah E. Stillman
David R.M. Davis
Asher M. Kerpp   dis
Clurrinder Nichols   dis
Richard Davis   exc 1855
Henry C. Coon
Henry Langworthy May 1852
Polly D. Dye   res   1855

Roselter Burdick   res
Lodusker D. Burdick   dis
Daniel Babcock
Erastus Nichols
Eveline Nichols
Adison Palmer Sep 12, 1852
Lorena Johnson   res   1853
Lucy Jane Stillman res 1853
Esther A. Dye   re 1855

p. 5

Lists of NAMES of RESIDENT MEMBERS dated July 28, 1855
Lincklaen NY

| NAMES | RESIDENT DISMISSED DECEASED | NAMES | RESIDIDENT DISMISSED DECEASED |

(date only for death)
(This section has incredibly poor spelling and penmanship.
V's, H's, and M's often indistinguishable.)

Persla Burdick
Thomas Stillman Jul 29,'55
Almeda Stillman dis May 25,'69
Dianny H Stillman   dis
Cyrus Cartwright dis Sep 9,'60
Julina M. Cartwright dis Sep 9,'60
Susannah Cartwright
Celinda Olin   dis
Sanford B. Stillman
Martha Burdick Ap 29, '66
Daniel C. Burdick
Henry C. Burdick rj Jul 12,'63
Clark Coon
William G. Crandall
Adeline Stillman dis
Abram Coon   dis
Thomas H. Burdick d. no date
Alzerda Cartwright dis Mar 16,'62
Kenyon B. Coon dis 1860
Maxson Stillman Mar 28,'57
Polly E. Burdick Oct 13, '55
Susan Burdick

Flavila Stillman
Benjamin H. Burdick Mar 9'56
Avery C. Stillman   dis
Olive Saunders   Jul'56
Benjamin S. Burdick
Abigail Stillman
Hannah B.C Cartwright
Martha Crumb
Lucy Olin Aug 17,'61
Howard Stone Dec 1860
Clarrisa Burdick
Jared Stillman   dis
Betsy Coon
Schuyler Olin
Sarah Ann Stillman   dis
Esther Coon   dis
Julian Marble
Martha A. Burdick
Samuel R. Stillman
Temperance L. Burdick
Jane Coon
Manervy Coon

p. 6
Sally A. Dye
Johaney H. Palmer
Clarinda Dye
David C. Coon   rj
Samuel Justice
Jane Stillman
Rosetta Nichols Jun 22,'56

Harriet Lyon Jul 9,'68
Mary Stillman   dis
Orlando Dye
Harriet Burdick
Lucinda Justice Oct 29 '66
Mary Ann Stillman   dis
Sarah L. Stillman

Nancy C. Stillman Nov 27,'56
Norman Burdick dis 1860
Kenyon Burdick Jr
Mary Ann Coon
Edward Burdick
Susan Stillman   dis
Cornealia R. Olin dis 1856
Martha R. Burdick
Elizabeth F Burdick
Orvil Stillman ad 1851
Benjamin Stillman   dis
Sarah E. Stillman
Erastus Nichols
Elvelina Nichols
Addison Palmer
Henry Langworthy Nov 18,'68
Lorena Johnson dis Oct 16, '63

Lpines Burdick dis 1860
Daniel Coon Sep 27,'56
Asa Coon   1857
Lydia Burdick
Sylvenus Burdick
Luanna Burdick
Martha P. Olin   dis 1860
Lucina Maine Dec 26,'65
D. R. M. Davis
Luis J. Burdick   ad   1852
Rosetta Burdick
Daniel L. Babcock
Clarinda Nichols
Henry C. Coon dis Ap '68
Lucy Jane Stillman
Polly D. Dye
Esther A. Dye

p. 7

Name	Admitted	Status
Jonathan H. Babcock	ad Sep '55	
Amos R. Cornwall	ad Sep Amos 1,'55;	then dis
Amy E. Burdick	ad Oct 28,'55	
Almira H. Burdick	ad Oct 28,'55	
Sophronia H. Burdick	ad Oct 28,'55	
Halsey Stillman	ad Mar 9, 1856;	dis Dec 1857
Welcome Burdick	" Jan 17, 1857;	rj Jul 12, 1863
Norman Olin	" " " "	dis Mar 4, 1863
Giles Johnson	" " " "	dis
Oscar Crandall	" " " "	
Ann E. Jones	" " " "	rj May 27, 1860
Elvira Johnson	" " " "	
Sarah Church	" " " "	
Charcelia Harvey	" " " "	
Chary Ingham	" Jan 21, 1857	
Sarah Burdick	" " " "	d. Jul 4, 1868
Francis Harvey	" " " "	
LaFayette Church	" " 25 "	rj May 10, 1863
Melissa Burdick	" " " "	
Villard L. Vilcox	" Apr 9, 1859	d. Feb 22, 1861
Benjamin H. Stillman	" May 7, 1855	dis May 23, 1868
Eld Lewis N Cottrell	" Jun 4, 1859	dis Apr 1860
Lucy M. Cottrell	see above	
Sybbil Vilcox	ad Aug 13, 1859	
William "	" " " "	
Andrew Parker	" Jun 2, "	d. Dec 25, 1862 in the hosp.
Lucy Burdick	" Oct 19, 1860	dis May 23, 1869
Henry Muncy	" " " "	d. Apr 9, 1863 in the hosp
Mary Eliza Stillman	bp Oct 19, 1860	
Martha Crandall	" " " "	
Sarah Jane Stillman	bp Mar 2, 1861	
Esther Muncy	" " " "	
James E. V. Backus	" May 18, 1861	dis Jun 1, 1861
Lucy A. Backus	bp May 18, 1861	dis Jun 1, 1861

Jesse Muncy	ad Jun 1, 1861	d. Feb 28, 1868
Jane E.P. Wilcox	" " " "	d Apr 4, 1865
Eld Thomas Fisher	" " " "	dis May 10, 1868
Eld Grace "	see above	
Adaline Stillman	bp Sep 14, 1861	
Emily Babcock	ad Dec 13, 1861	
Emma Stillman	bp Apr 9, 1864	
Emily Burdick	bp " 23 "	
Nlala Crandall	bp " " "	
Genett Burdick	bp " " "	
Phineas Burdick	ad Nov 20, "	d. Jan 13, 1870

p. 8

APR 8, 1865

Joseph L. Rogers   Celinda L. Rogers

1866

Eld Amos W. Coon   ad Dec 14   Annie Coon ad Dec 14

1867

Eunice Coon   bp Jan 26   Sarah Justice bp Jan 26
Samuel Allen   bp May 4   Arminda Allin ad Jun 21
Eld Halsey Stillman ad Nov 24   Pamilla Stillman ad Nov 24

1868

Rubin Crumb   ad Jun 6   Eunice Crumb   ad Jun 6

APR 10, 1869   BAPTISED

George T. Stillman   George R. Stillman
Adelia A. Stillman   Charlie Burdick
Caroline E. Burdick   Adelbert Crumb

APRIL 24, 1869   BAPTISED

Grant Burdick   Dewitte Burdick
Mary Burdick   Lucy Crumb
Almina Coon   Caroline Olin
Alida Muncy   Avery Nichols
Alfred Coon   Elizabeth Justice bpMay 22
Frank Davis   Alverda Justice
Norman Smith   Floid Stillman
Eugene Johnson   Kinyon B. Coon restored
Clarinda Coon   bp May 22
Ervilla Marshall ad May 8 First Day Baptist Church

Lincklaen 1847-1871   Vol 2   CRR 19x.106 NY Box vault
IMS: 1993   (poor penmanship & spelling)

RECORDS of the SDB CHURCH in LINCKLEAN
Chenango Co. NY

List of RESIDENT and NONRESIDENT MEMBERS
(If death date, no other notation given)

| NAMES | DATES | NAMES | DATES |

p. 1
Vasta Burdick   Oct 31 '71
Flavilla Stillman   NR May'80
Abigail Stillman   Jan 23'77
Martha Crumb   July 2,'81
Sanford B Stillman   Oct 15'72
Daniel C Burdick   Aug 26,'85
William J Crandall   Jun 30,'81
Sarah A. Stillman   Feb 8,'80
Martha Burdick   Feb 23,'72
Clarinda Dye   dis Mar 23,'70
Orlando Dye   dis Dec 1870
Harriet Burdick   dis Mar 8,'76
Samuel Justus   dis May 15,18??
Lydia Burdick   Oct 20,'79
Sylvanus Burdick   dis Oct 15,'70
Martha B. Burdick   dis Mar 8,'76
Orvil L. Stillman   dis Aug '76
Rosetta Burdick   dis Oct 25,'70

Susannah Cartwright   dead
B.S. Burdick   exc
Clarissa Burdick dead
Clark Coon May 17,'81
Betsey Coon Nov 16,'87
Schuyler Olin Mar 8, 91
Juliaann Marble dis '77
Wealthy A. Burdick dis
Jane Coon Jul 8, '89
Minerva Coon Marble
Sarah S. Stillman
Mary Ann Coon
Edward Burdick
Luanna Burdick   exc
Lewis J. Burdick
Elizabeth Burdick dead
Sarah E. Hendee Dec 6,'75

p. 2
Erastus Nichols   Jul 16,'80
Elvalina Nichols excommunicated
Lucy J. Stillman   dis Apr. 4,'71
Jonathan H. Babcock   dis 1876
Sophronia Burdick   Feb 13, 1927
Elmira H. Burdick Craft   dead
Merselia Harvey   dis Jul 7,'75
Sibiel Wilcox   1884
Mary E. Stillman   dis Sep 15,'79
Martha B. Crandall   dis Jun '73
Adeline Stillman   dis Aug '76
Emily Babcock   Dec 8,'82
Joseph S. Rogers   May 17,'72
Celinda Rogers   dis Feb 8,'73
Samuel Allen   Nov 24,'83
Eunice Crumb   dis Jan 30,'75
George T. Stillman   dis Mar '79
George R. Stillman   dis Jun'85
Charles Burdick   exc Sep'73

Clarinda Nichols
Welcome A. Palmer exc
Polly D. Dye dis 1878
Daniel R.M. Davis dead
Amey E. Burdick dis '76
Elvira Johnson
Frances Harvey
William Wilcox
Esther Muncy
Emmaline Stillman
Janet Burdick dis Mar'79
Annie Coon dis Mar '72
Eunice Coon dis Mar '72
Sarah Justus Oct '80
Reuben Crumb Mar 29,'79
Caroline E. Burdick excom
Adelbert Crumb   dis
DeWitt Burdick
Grant Burdick

p. 3
Mary Burdick   Jul 8,'72
Lucy Crumb exc   Nov 12,'71
Elyda Muncy   dis for leaving Sabbath, joining 1st day church
Franklin Davis   rj May 26,'72
Eugene Johnson   dis Jan'79

Elmina Coon
Caroline M. Olin

Avery Nichols
Alfred M. Coon

Norman Smith   Dec 25, 72
Kenyon B. Coon   May 9, '89
Ervilla Marshall   dis '79
Elizabeth Jastis   Aug 12, '79
Kenyon Burdick   Feb 8, '82
Amanda T. Stillman   Aug 10, '79
Emely Burdick   dis 1881
Sarah J. Stillman   dis Sep '71
Daniel C. Babcock   dis '84
Susan Burdick   May 29, '80
Martha C. Burdick   ad Feb '72   d. May 7, 1888

Edverdo Jastus
Floyd F. Stillman
Oscar A. Crandall
Clarinda Coon
Lydia T. Burdick   dead
Samuel R. Stillman
Lohansy H. Burdick   exc
Amos W. Coon   dis Jan '71
Arminda Allen
Phebe J. Crandall   dis

p. 4
Luke C. Burdick   bp Feb 25, '72 by Eld Joshua Clark;   d. Feb 28, '74
Alphus Hendee   bp "   "   "   "   "   "   dp keeps Sunday
Amos Justice   bp Feb 25, '72 by Eld Joshua Clark
Elda Marble   "   "   "   "   "   "   "
Lydia Smith   "   "   "   "   "   "   "   d. Oct 27, '83
Edgar Coon   bp "   "   "   "   "
Josephine S. Coon   bp Mar 2, 1872; dis
Schuyler Coon received by experience 1872;   dis Dec 1979 Cansas (KS ?)
Caroline Coon   see above
Isaac Smith   ad Apr 1872;   d. 1888
Maria Coon   bp Dec 21, '72
Lydia A. Wills   dis; dead
Harriet H. Burdick   bp Dec '75; dis
Ida Davis   bp Dec '75; excom
Amelia Coon   bp Dec '75
Margaret Wright
Laverne Davis   bp Dec '75
Arvilla Burdick   bp Dec 1, '76
Jenna Stillman   "   "   "   " ; d. Feb 14, 1884
Delina B. Wilcox   ad Feb 19, 1876
Halsey Stillman   ad Apr '77   dis
Amelia Stillman   ad Jul '77   dis
Schuyler S. Coon   ad Mar '81   joined church in Cansas (KS?)
Benjamin H. Stillman   ad Apr 16, '81
Jennie M. Stillman   ad May 27, '82; d. Feb 14, '89
Varnum W. Coon   ad Sept 16, '82; d. May 28, '90
Nancy Coon   "   "   "   "   d. Jul 25, '90
Leon D. Burdick   "   "   "   "
Louis H. Burdick "   "   "   "
Celina Johnson   Oct 14, '82 (No indication what date is for.)
Willie Coon   "   "   "   "   "   "   "   "   "
Jennie Burdick   Nov 11   "   "   "   "   "   "   "
Henry D. Burdick   "   "   "   by letter
Cornelia Burdick   see above
David Finch   Jan 7, '83 (No indication what date is for.)
Amanda Justice   ad Nov 10, '86
Celinda Rogers   ad Mar 8, '86

CRR 19x.103   NY Box   vault
Lincklaen   1871-96   IMS: 1993

TRUXTON 1824–c.1943
also called CUYLER HILL Cortland Co., NY
Sabbath keepers in area in 1815
organized 1824–c1943 with 57 members mostly from DeRuyter

Dea. Zacheus Maxson-DeRuyter dis
Benjamin C. Maxson 1839
James Muncy
Aaron Fox
Matthew M. Crandall restored 1836; dis
Seymour Hamilton
David V. Wells dis Nov 1, 1834
Ezra Burdick restored '31, dis 1834
Caleb W. Church dis 1839
Barber Cardner Jr. rj
Benjamin Maxson dis
Isaac Philips rj 1834
Thomas Pye rj
Rawssl Richmond 1835
Zacheus R. Maxson dis
Benjamin Clark Maxson -RI
Sarah Hamilton rj
Sarah Pye rj
Martha Maxson dis
Pricilla Richmond dis 1838
Thankful Richmond dis 1838
Mary Pye rj
Prudence Crandall dis
Mary Irish
Luanna Burdick dis 1847
Annis Burdick
Harris Church dis 1835
Eliza A. Maxson dis Lincklaen
Malviena Colegrove rj 1836
Sally A. Irish dis 1835
Luke Crandall-RI d. Nov 11, 1838
Martha Crandall-RI deceased
Temperence Crandall-DeRuyter dis
Alexander Campbell-Adams'34; dis Sep'87
Elie S. Colegrove-DeRuyter
Lot Scrivens
Betsey Colegrove rj
Stephen Cardner
Edwin Church
Susan Church dis Sep 1834
Daniel J. Burdick Oct 23, 1834
Amanda Irish deceased
Martha Emily Maxson
Sally Maxson deceased
Eliza Cardner Oct 25, 1834
James Burdick Nov 1, 1834
Synthuan Wright restored Sep 14, 1839
Arminda Muncy Jul 1835
Jared Stillman joined Lincklaen

Dea. Barber Carder
Elie Colegrove rj
Nathan Vorght rj
Jacob Seamons
Elias Irish
Russel G. Burdick
David Cardner rj 1839
John Pye rj
William Allen rj
V. M. Burdick
Elisha Wells
Daniel Richmond rj
Benjamin Burdick d.
Jason Burdick rj
Syntha Warte
Polly Church dis 1834
Patty Burdick rj '36
Anna Pye rj
Martha Sheldon
Judith Colegrove rj
Esther Muncy
Susan Coon-RI
Susan Irish
Lucinda Burdick dis
Catharine Irish
Prudence Allen
Mary Cardner
Rowland Crandall-RI
Kinyon Cardner
Margaret Cardner
Silas Davis-Scott
Polly Cooley rj
Betsey Wells dis 1835
Clarinda Campbell dis
Deodamia Colgrove
Harriet Scrivens
Ephraim Cardner rj
Matthew Cardner
Mary Church dis 1836
Polly Cardner 1839
Melissa Burdick
Eliza Irish
Angeline Maxson
Phineas C. Burdick
Thomas Maxson
Matthew Maxson
Freeman Maxson rj
Zexvell Campbell
Anna Campbell

Roxyan Burdick
David Wells rj
William Burdick rj 1832
Zebediah Burdick 1837
Rev. Benjamin B. Maxson
Eli S. Colegrove 1838
Judith Colgrove restored Sep 14, 1834
Sally B. Colgrove 1838
Lot Crandall-Brookfield
Patty Crandall-Brookfield
Henry Rogers-Waterford, CN
Ephraim Curtis-Preston
Susan Curtis-Preston
Lydia Burdick
David Colgrove
Jacob Gardner
Larry Burdick d. Mar 1848
Mary Rogers-Close Communion 1st Baptist Church, Waterford CN; dis
Abner Wannen-Free Will Baptist, Stephentown, Rensselear Co.; dis
Judith Colgrove d. Sep 14, 1839
Eli Colgrove restored Sep 1, 1839   deceased
Elias Rogers-Friendship Church Oct 20, 1834   dis
Content Rogers   see above
Sollomon S. Coon-Lincklaen
Susan Coon-DeRuyter
Minerva Moone bp Oct '39; exc May 14, 1849
Amy Phillips   see above
Lydia C. Maxson   see above
Arzaville Colgrove   see above
Orson C. Colgrove   exc Nov 19, 1848
Martha Moone   exc Nov 19, 1848
Prudence Mooney   Jan 1841
Luke M. Mooney   Mar 1842
Orrin M. Elmore   Mar 1842
Arza Muncy Mar 1842
Alpina Muncy Mar 1842
Clarrissa A. Burdick May 1847
Arelia Muncy Feb 5, 1848
Emily James exc Nov 19, 1848
Isiah G. Maxson d. Apr 2, 1879

Huldah Wells   dis
George Crandall dis
Elias B. Irish
Albert Muncy 1837
Aemyza Muncy
Janutice Wannen
Stephen G. Wannen
Julianner Wannen   bp
Prudence Ann Moone
Sarah Moone d. 1849
Edson A. D. Cardner
Luisa Burdick
Spencer Burdick
Deodamy Colgrove
Albert C. Maxson
Polly Cardner

Lydia Burdick
Deodamy Colgrove
David Colgrove
Albert C. Maxson
Jacob Gardner
Larry Burdick d. Mar. 1848
Polly Cardner

CRR 1970.4 vault
Truxton (Cuyler Hill) SDB Records   1824- 1845
Penmanship was difficult; reader should allow for
    discrepencies.   IMS: 1993

First Anniversary
of the
CUYLER Sabbath School
Thursday Evening, May 19, 1864

Programme

Oscar J. Irish	Julia Burdick
Clark Johnson	Adell Phillips
Nancy Burdick	Jemima Culver
Lilly Green	Wells Cardner
Addie Burdick	Newel Muncy
Eugene Phillips	Jennette Burdick
Wells Carder	Frank Garner
C. H. Brown	Jane Coon
Isabel Coon	Harriet Tuttle
Emogene Cardner	Elsie Irish

CRR 1970.4   vault
Truxton, NY (Cuyler Hill) SDB Church Records

IMS: 1993

PRESTON
1817-1831   1900-c1910
Chenango Co., NY

Constituent Members

Davis Rogers - fr Waterford CN	Ethan Rogers - fr Waterford CN
Davis Rogers, Jr "	Silas Rogers "
Hannah Rogers " - deceased	Sally Rogers "
Polly Rogers "	Sally Rogers 2nd "
Eld David Davis fr DeRuyter - deceased	Lydia Rogers-dec. "

Other Members

Clark T. Rogers	Washington Truman
Jennet Rogers	Sarah Truman
Mary Rogers - rj	Nathan T. Truman - dis
Fanny Rogers - dis Alfred	Luke Lanphier - dis Scott
Nancy Rogers - dis Alfred	Rebekah Potter
Fedilia Moon - rj	Sarah Barber - dis Scott
Holly Maxson	Judith Maxson
Ephranina Babcock	Amy Babcock
Abel Babcock	Daniel Babcock
Martha Clark	Ephraim Rogers
Sammuel Barber	Chloe Rogers
Polly Lanphier	Anna Truman
Dea. Wait Clark - rj	Warren Hooper
Polly Greffing - dis Otselic	Luanny Phillips
Abigail Clark - deceased	Nathan Rogers
John Truman - dis	Phebe Rogers
William Clark	Ethan Rogers Jr
Jesse Rogers	Ephraim Rogers
Susanna Curtis - dis	Cynthy Truman - dis
Sally Ann Rogers - dis	Clarresy Truman
Ephraim Curtis - dis	Fanny Rogers
Judith Lester	Roby Welmath
Aseneth Truman	Amos Rogers
Meriah Yeomans	Elpha Lewis
Mary Ann Clark	Asenath Truman 2nd
Sophia Truman	Hannah Rogers
Jennet Rogers 2nd	Phebe Rogers 2nd
Aden Rogers	Polly Rogers 2nd
Sally Ann Williams	

CRR 19x.101   vault
Preston NY Church Records

IMS: 1993

NORWICH   Chenango Co NY
1879-c1915

organized Dec 6, 1879 by Eld. L.C. Rogers
nine constutuent members
No primary records extant

IMS: 1993

ITHACA
Thomkin Co.   NY
1883-c1910
No primary records extant   IMS:1993

NEWPORT
Herkimer Co. 1838-c1910
17 members
SDB Mmemorial Vol 1, p. 142   IMS:1993

OTSELIC (South)
Chenango Co. NY 1838-c.1915

"Inscriptions from monuments in the Seventh Day Hollow Cemetery in the town of Otselic. It is located three miles south on the east side of Rt. 26 opposite the intersection with Bucks Brook. These were copied in 1961 by Mrs. Ernest Macall and Mrs. Henry Card of Otselic."

ALLEN	Fred - 1865-1930
	Lillie - 1872-1949
BASSETT	Darius - b Sept 19, 1820; d May 31, 1906
	Harriet w/o Darius - b Nov 28, 1821; d May 10, 1900
CHURCH	Samuel C. - b Jan 16, 1818; d Apr 14, 1890;CO. I,IReg,NYSU
THOMPSON	Susannah w/o Samuel Church - b Jan 26, 1821; d Nov 11, 1890
CHURCH	Flora d/o Samuel & Susannah - d Sep 2, 1868, 2 yrs & 18 days
	Silas - d Oct 24, 1867, 3 weeks & 4 days
	also infant children of Fayette & Sarah Church
	Franklin L. - d Dec 22, 1883, 41 yrs
	Charles H. s/o Thelisma & Mercy - d Oct 20, 1866, 15 yrs
	Alva B. s/o Thelisma - d Oct 7, 1867, 31 yrs;GAR Post 456
	Thelisma - d Nov 3, 1869;, 57 yrs
COAKLEY	Almon D. - d May 17, 1888, 27 yrs
	William W. - b Sep 9, 1838; d Oct 26, 1915; Co. G 114 Reg
	Reg. NY.S. Vols. GAR Post 456
	Francis - b 1858, d 1844
	Ribin - b 1889 no death date given
	Lizzie - b 1895 no death date given
	Abigail - b. Sep 26, 1824; d Jan 6, 1866
CRUMB	Henry M. - b 1836; d 1910
	Emma L. w/o Henry - b 1846; d 1908
	Walter D. - b 1878; d 1906
DERMOTT	John - b 1817; d 1888
	Mary w/o John - 1817; d 1877
DYE	John P. - b 1854; d 1917
	Emily M. - b 1861 no death date given
	John C. - b 1896; d 1919
FIFIELD	Samuel - d Oct 13, 1871, 80 yrs
	Almira w/o Samuel - d Sep 22, 1886, 90 yrs
	Ira A. - d Sep 9, 1870, 49 yrs
	Ira - d Aug 13, 1867, 70 yrs
	Irena w/o Ira - d Jan 15, 1872, 32 yrs, 3 mo, 27 days
HIGGINS	Mary E. F. - d Nov 10, 1907, 78 yrs
HOOK	Benjamin - b Dec 25, 1799 England;d Jan 19, 1886,68yrs-21d
HART	Milo B. - b 1829, d 1899
	Sally L. w/o Milo - b 1841; no death date given
HOWARD	Martin B. - d FEb 11, 1882, 95 yrs
	Betsey w/o Martin - d Mar 14, 1873, 85 yrs
HUTCHINSON	James - b 1781; d 1873
	Martha w/o James - b 1791; d 1863
HUMPHREY	Thelma - b 1914; d 1921
	Kenneth S. - b 1902; d 1929
	Mona d/o Will & Lena- b July 30, 1907; d JUn 10, 1910
	Phyllis I.O. - b 1900; d 1915
	Lena Opal - b 1900; d 1917

73

	Lena Pearl w/o Will - b 1878; d 1917
KINGSLEY	Palmer G. - d Sep 28, 1879, age 71-4-9
	Susan Braiman w/o Palmer - d Mar 13, 1881, age 71-1-11
	Marek D. - b 1846, d 1919
	John J. - b 1846, d 1882; Co. I, NY Cav. (20)
NOURSE	Clinton K. - b. 1842, d 1914; Co. K, 14 NY Vols. GAR Post 456
	Henrietta Church w/o Clinton - b 1847, d 1914
PHILLIPS	Esek - Jun 30, 1866, age 72 yrs
	Ann w/o Esek - d Oct 31, 1887, age 86 yrs
	Daniel - d Apr 28, 1883, age 42 yrs
	Charlie s/o Daniel & Mary - July 15, 1881, age 2 mos
PRICE	Ruth d/o P.H. & A. H. (or M.) no dates given
	Mary - Illegible
	John - Illegible
	John J. - d Feb. 18, 1902, age 68 yrs-6mo.
	Asenath - d Mar 23, 1923, age 87 yrs-6 mo.
	Cora N. d/o J.J. & A. - d Apr 9, 1862, age 3-4-28
	E.B. - b 1868 no death date given
	Dora L. w/o E. B. - b 1862 no death date given
	Ella B. d/o E. B. & Dora L. - b 1898, d 1898
	Claudie s/o J.J. & M. A. - d Aug 15, 1881, 1 yr
	Malinda A. w/o Jelsworth - d Sep 8, 1883, 22 yrs
POWERS	Mary w/o Henry Rogers - d Mar 17, 1851, 67 yrs
ROGERS	Emmett C. - b Nov 8, 1861, d Jan 5, 1931
	Bertha C. w/o Emmett C. - b Aug 30, 1863, d Feb 9, 1911
	Charles A. - b 1829, d 1895
	Mary E. - b 1856, d 1861
	John H. - b 1853, d 1905
	Nathaniel S. Illegible
SOULE	Joel - d Aug 15, 1885, 65 yrs
STILLMAN	Olive - 1857-1935
	Minnie - Sep 9, 1925, age 12 days
SHERMAN	Oliver - d Sep 11, 1870, age 68 yrs & 11 mos.
TRUMAN	Thomas - d Nov 23, 1891, age 67
	Elizabeth w/o Thomas - d May 29, 1908, age 82 yrs
	Twins s/o & d/o Thomas - d Feb 10, 1865, age 1 day
	Edgar only s/o Ed. & A.M. - Nov 14, 1879, age 1-1-5
NORRIS	Illegible between Fifield & Truman stones
TRUMAN	John - 1807-1880
	Sarah A. - 1815-1870
	Nathan - 1826-1907
	Angelet w/o Nathan - 1833-1918
	Willie - 1860-1864
	Catherine w/o Thomas - d Sep 6, 1867, age 70-7-6
CARD	Abigail - b Sep 26, 1824, d Jan 6, 1866 (This is the Abigail Coakley on p. 39. Her correct name was omitted.)
TRUMAN	Mary E. - d Mar Mar 1878, 45 yrs
	Sylvester - b Oct 17, 1883, d May 2, 1901
	Willie s/o Nathan & Angelet - d Oct 17, 1884, 12 yrs-8 mo-10d
	Dudley W. - b Jan 31, 1822, d Feb 10, 1898
	F. A. Roxana w/o Dudley - b Mar 16, 1827, d Mar 16, 1911
	Letta (Leota) adopted s/o D. & R. Truman - d Apr 26, 1878 age 9 mo-7 da

fr TREE TAlkS Chanago Co.   IMS: 1993

FIRST VERONA
Oneida Co   1820-
Verona Mills; Blackman Corners Rd SDB Church

Constituent Members

Thomas Williams
Robert Williams
Henry Williams
Ray Williams
Elisha Maxson
Amy Williams
Henry Williams
Ester Williams
Desire Williams
Zilpha Williams
Sarah Williams
Benjamin Davis

Daniel Williams Jr
George H. Williams
Joshua Williams
Wait Williams
Amey Williams
Neoma Williams dec
Elizabeth Maxson
Freelove Williams
Jehobod Williams
Calleb Barton
Amey Hassard
Mary Williams

April 15, 1820

Isvey Whitford
Daniel Williams 3rd
Susannah Greene
Jeny Greene
Nancy Davis
Henry Williams
Barbery Williams
Freelove Williams Jr

Calib Greene
Daniel Williams 4th
Pardon Williams
John Greene
Mary Williams
Thomas Williams
Mary Williams

April 22, 1820

William Green
Silloma Williams
Nancy Green
Alva Green
Sandford Green
Benjamin Davis Jr
Mary Williams w/o Thomas
Elinor Davis

Margaret Williams
Soffy Williams
Joseph Williams
Joseph Davis
Sally Williams
Caroline Green
William Davis
Mary Williams w/o Daniel

Later List With Some Pages Frayed Away

Thomas Williams
Daniel Williams Jr
Henry Williams
Freelove Williams
Sesive Williams
Amy Hassard
Caleb Greene   rj
Ira Greene
William Greene
Margaret Williams 2nd
Joseph Williams
Joseph Davis
William Davis   rj
Mary Williams w/o Thomas
Mary Williams w/o Daniel
Elinor Davis dec

Robert Williams
George H. Williams
Mary Williams
Ester Williams dec
Sarah Williams
Daniel Williams 4th
Susannah Greene
John Greene
Nancy Greene
Salome Williams
Alva Greene
Sandford Greene rj
Sally Williams
Elmer Davis   dec
Carline Greene
Gideon Williams

Diah Lawton	Joseph Lawton
Thomas Perry	Nancy Perry
Sophia Williams	Pardon Williams
Amy Williams	James Morgan
Sally Williams w/o Henry	Mary Morgan
Lucetta Williams	Eunice Vonter
Bersheba Williams	Robert Williams 2nd
Sally Davis	Esther Williams
Elcy Williams	Calesta Williams
Parley Conger	Harison G. Williams
Eliza Williams	Thomas Perry
Amanda Williams	Russel Saunders
Bethiah West	John R. Satterlee
Joshua Williams Jr	Permilla Saterley
Daniel B. Tull	Oliva Tull
Mary West	Adilia West
Emaly West	Jabia West
Elizabeth Gray	Marietta Peckham
Ester Peckham	Samuel P. Nash
Deborah R. Williams	Zilpha Ann Williams
Lyda Davis	Henry S. Burdick
Mather An Burdick	Joseph H. Hazzard
Pelina Davis	Jerry Perry
Sophrona Green	Margaret Green
Amanda N. Williams	Mary E. Williams
George Banester	Margaret Coil
George Davis	Stephen Davis
Albert Joel	Charles Green dis
Widdow Mary Williams	Lydia Perry
Mary Perry	Arriminta West
Reone Mary Hadden	Susan M. Davis
Enock K. Crandall	Holsea H. Baker
Robert Davman	Rachel Oaks
Hiram Sherman	Wells Kenyon
Abby Susan Kenyon	Remina Dorman
Jamina Lutes	Nancy A. Harris
Barbara M. Kenyon	Adilia E. Kenyon
Roxannah Green	Rachel L. Oaks
Lydia Kinyon	Permilla L. Williams
Eld. John Kinyon dec 1838	Belinda Williams
Francis Williams	Joseph Lawton
Joseph Lawton Jr	Nancy Lawton
Joanna Lawton	Anna Davis
Caroline Hassard	Lamson B. Lawton
Ansah Corwin	Robert T. Lawton
Franklin H. Williams	Augustus B. Harris
Joseph H. Hassard	Daniel Davis
Orvil A. Williams	Joseph Davis
Clark Davis	Ebenezer Hilson
Amy Lear	Ester Williams
Jemima Gardner	Charles M. Lewis
Margaret Gruostell rj May 10, 1810	Whitford G. Green
Edward Williams	Amos Williams
John Williams	Henry Burdick

Martha Burdick   Angeline Williams
Sarah Ann Mumford   Henry B. Lewis
Eliza Perry   Susan Williams

The Book of Records of the Sabbathkeeping Brethren
in the Town Rome and Verona NY
Nov 17, 1809-Feb 10, 1841
CRR 1980.8.1   vault   IMS: 1993

MEMBERS   Mar 18, 1841

Dea. Thomas Williams - d Jul 15, 1863, 96 yrs
Dea. Daniel Williams Jr - d Sep 9, 1863, 90 yrs
Robert Williams - d Jan 28, 1867, 91 yrs
George H. Williams - dec
Henry Williams - dec
Wait Williams - dis
Elisha Maxson - dec
Amy Williams - dec
Elizabeth Maxson - d Mar 14, 1885
Mercy Williams - d Aug 21, 1870
Freelove Williams - dec
Desire Williams - dec
Joshua Williams - d Jan 2, 1835, 58 yrs
Sarah Williams - dec
Henry Williams Jr - dis
Freelove Williams - NR; dis 188?; 89 yrs
Daniel Williams 3rd - d 1883
Susannah Green - d Aug 1872
Ira Green - Mar 30, 1887, 80 yrs 4 mo
William Green - dec
Saloma Williams - d Jun 14, 1853
Nancy Green - d 1857
Joseph Williams - d 1866
Benjamin Davis Jr - dis
Caroline Green Marsh - dec
Nancy Green w/o Ira - d Mar 8, 1885; 79 yrs
Sophia Williams - dis
Amy Williams - rj May 22, 1852
Ichabod Williams - dec
Mary Williams - dec
Barsheba Williams - dis
Robert Williams 2nd - d 1883
Sally Davis - dis
Esther Williams - d Apr 14, 1845
Calista Williams Jones - 1892, 82 yrs
Mary E. Williams Harris - dis Apr 22, 1883
Permilla Williams Crandall - NR; dec
Lucretia Williams Bennett - d 1876
Thomas J. Williams - rj
Moses B. Lawrence - NR; dec
Armand Leribbins - dis

Martha Williams - dec
Sarah Hazard Wordsworth - dis May 1883
Abby Hazard Williams - NR; dec
Harrison J. Williams - d Mar 29, 1852
Eliza A. Lewis - dis
Lucinda Leribbins - dis
Fanny Williams - dis
Jacob Burdick - dis
Mary Lawrence - dis
Susannah Williams Larkin - dec
Esther Green Cagwin - d Nov 1885
Daniel L. Williams - d May 13, 1901
Daniel B. Tull - NR; dp
Olive Tull - NR; dp
Deborah B. Williams Bennett - d Feb 20, 1904
Zilpha Ann Williams Davis - dis
Lydia Davis - dis Jan 29, 1865; restored same day
Henry L. Perry - d Jan 1889; 80 yrs
Sophrona Green Babcock - dis
Margaret Green Langworthy - dis Feb 4, 1872
Amanda M. Perry - dec
Mary Williams - d Mar 1886
George Banister - NR; dis Aug 24, 1884
Margaret Coil Chaplin - d Nov 7, 1903
Thomas Perry - d Mar 1888
George Davis - NR; d Aug 1881
Stephen R. Davis - rj
Albert Powel - dis
Wid. Mary Williams - d 1850
Lydia Perry - d Nov 1887
Mary Perry - d 1884
Enoch H. Crandall - dis; dec
Robert Dorman - dec
Rachel Oaks - dec
Hiram Sherman - d. Jun 13, 1863
Wells Kenyon - dec
Abby Susan Kenyon - dis
Rumina Dorman - dec
Jemima Lutes Burdick - dec
Nancy A. Harris - rj Oct 1, 1843
Barbara M Kenyon - dec
Adelia E. Kenyon - rj Sep 18, 1853
Rosannah Green - rj Oct 1, 1843
Rachel D. Oaks - dec
Lydia Kenyon - dec
Permilla S. Williams - dis
Francis R. Williams - dp
Joseph Lawton - dec
Joseph Lawton Jr - dis Mar 23, 1856
Nancy Lawton - d Jun 1854
Anna Davis - dis
Caroline Hazard Lea - rj
Alanson B. Lawton - dis
Anson Cowels - rj

Robert T. Lawton - Jan 22, 1848
Franklin H. Williams - d Nov 18, 1866
Augustus P. Harris - dis
Joseph H. Hazard - rj Sep 21, 1845
Daniel Davis - d Sep 1, 1902
Orville A. Williams - d 1910
Joseph B. Davis - bp; dis
Clark Davis - NR; dec
Ebenezer C. Stilson - bp; dec
Jemima Gardner - bp; d 1876
Charles M. Lewis - ad; dis
Whitford Green - bp; dis
Edward Williams - bp; rj Mar 4, 1852
Amos Williams - bp; rj 1850; restored 1865
John Williams - bp; dis
Henry Burdick - bp; rj
Martha Burdick - bp; rj 1874
Angeline Williams Warmis - bp; dec
Sarah Ann Mumford - bp; dis
Henry B. Lewis - dis
Eliza Perry Sherman - bp; d Dec 1877
Susan M. Williams - bp; NR; d Feb 18, 1869
Parley Conger - bp; NR; dp
Charles Lear - bp; dis
Alfred R. Lawton - bp; rj
Hiram B. Eades - bp; rj
Desire Eades - bp; d. Oct, 1890
Reubin Jersel - bp; NR; dp
Nancy M. Lawton Williams - bp; dis Mar 23, 1854
John W. Green - restored; d Jun 1881
Mariah J. Holt - bp; dis Apr 1854
David P. Marsh - bp; dis
Harriet P. Green - bp; d Mar 17, 1897
Caroline E. Holcomb - bp; rj Mar 20, 1846
Alfred R.K. Bennett - bp; d May 5, 1900
Elizabeth H. Lewis - bp Aug 12, 1844; dis
Tacy Williams - ad Aug 31, 1844
Henry B. Lewis - ad Sep 14, 1844
William Davis - ad Nov 9, 1844; d 1900
Russel Witter - ad Oct 25, 1845; dec
Mrs. Sally Witter - ad Oct 25, 1845; dec
Eld. Christopher Chester - ad Feb 11, 1848; dis Apr 1854
Oliver Sherman - bp Jun 1848; dis Nov 10, 1855
Olive Chester - ad Sep 1848; dis Apr 1854
Morris Langworthy - ad Apr 25, 1851; dis
Dea. Martin Willcox - ad Ap 26, 1851; d Jan 29, 1856
Mehital Willcox - ad Apr 26, 1851; dis 1856
Ruth Shattuck - ad Apr 26, 1851; dis 1856
Farozina Willcox - ad Ap 16, 1851; dis 1856
Mary Ann Williams w/o Franklin - ad May 10, 1851; rj 1884
Mary Ann Williams - ad May 10, 1851; rj
Martha Chester Perry - dec 1893
Margaret Williams - restored Apr 28, 1851; NR; dis
Martha6 Lawrence - ad May 19, 1850; NR; dis; dec

Mary Ann Green - bp Feb 20, 1853; dis
Eliza L. Perry Maxson - bp Feb Feb 20, 1853; dis
Cynthia L. Sherman - bp Feb 20, 1853; NR; dec
George W. Gardner - bp Feb 20, 1853; NR; dis 1858
Washington Perry - bp Feb 20, 1853; rj
Elizabeth Ann Williams - bp Feb 26, 1853; dis
Mary A. Gardner Allen - bp Feb 26, 1853
Permilla Marsh - bp Feb 26, 1853; dec
Susan M. Chester - bp Feb 26, 1853; dis Apr 185(?)
Oscar M. Williams - bp Feb 26, 1853; dec 189(?)
Thomas O. Gardner - bp Feb 26, 1953; dec
Barnabas Raymond - bp Feb 26, 1853; rj Sep 28, 1862
Susan Witter Peckham - bp Mar 5, 1853; rj
Lisa Lawton Witter - bp Mar 5, 1853; dis Mar 25, 1854
Ichabod Williams Gardner - bp Mar 5, 1853; d 1896
Frances Williams - bp Mar 6, 1853; NR; rj
Albert M. Clark - ad May 1854; NR; d 19??
Phebe M. Clark - ad May 1854; NR; d 1909
Albert Babcock - ad May 1854; dis
David P. Curtis - ad Nov 1, 1854; dis
Cordelia A. Curtis - ad Nov 1, 1854; dis
Abel G. Lewis - ad Jun 23, 1855
Martha Lewis w/o Abel - ad Jun 23, 1855
Caroline S. Green Stark - ad Jul 1, 1855
Wealthy Williams - ad Jul 1, 1855; d Jan 18, 1859
Fanny L. Perry - bp Aug 1, 1856; rj
Caroline S. Williams - bp Jun 21, 1856; d Jan 18, 1894
Julia Stebbins - bp Feb 14, 1857; dis
William Griffith - bp Feb 14, 1857; dp
Ellen Babcock - bp Feb 14, 1857; rj
Harriet E. Lewis - bp Feb 22, 1857; NR; dis 1866
Julia A. Bennett - bp Feb 22, 1857; d Apr 15, 1890
Eliza Ann Green (younger) - bp Feb 22, 1857; rj
Lucinda Marsh - bp Feb 22, 1857; dis
Emily Lea - bp Feb 22, 1857; dis
Susan Davis - ad 1857; d Sep 2, 1906
Robert Davis - bp 1857; rj
Albert Williams - bp 1857; dec
Alfred Williams - bp 1857; dis Feb 17, 1866
Theodore A. Perry - bp Mar 21, 1857; suspended (crossed out)
Antoinette Burdick Edwards - bp Mar 21, 1857; dec
Frances Allen - bp Mar 21, 1857; rj
Eliza Cagwin - bp Mar 21, 1857; dec
Samuel P. Marsh - restored Mar 29, 1857; rj Nov 29, 1868
Eld. Chs. M. Lewis - ad Oct 27, 1860; dis Apr 18, 1863
Eliza A. Lewis - see above
Mary E. Williams w/o John - bp Jun 1, 1861; dis Feb 17, 1866
Maria E. Sherman - bp Nov 23, 1861; dis
Zacheus T. Burdick - ad Mar 1862; dis
Charles Babcock - bp Feb 15, 1862; dis 1876
Charles Woodworth - bp Feb 15, 1862; dis 1883
Hamilton Babcock - bp Mar 8, 1862; rj
William Cogwin - bp Mar 8, 1862; dp
Francis Cogwin - bp Mar 8, 1862; dp

Frederick Almon - bp Feb 22, 1862; dec
Sarah Adelia Jones Lewis - ad Apr 26, 1862; dec
Eld. J. Bennett Clark - ad Jun 6, 1863; dis
Eunice Clark - see above
B.F. Stillman - ad Jul 4, 1863; dis
Harriet F. Stillman - see above
David H. Davis, China missionary - bp Sep 1863; dec 1915
Susan Ann Leonard - bp Jan 1864; dec 1886
Eld. A. Campbell - ad May 27, 1866; dis
Mrs. A. Campbell - ad Mar 28, 1868; dec
Frances Campbell Whitford - ad Mar 28, 1868; dec
Angela M.B. Campbell - ad Mar 28, 1868; dec
Flora Green Palmiter - bp Mar 28, 1868
Eddy Lea - bp May 8, 1869; dis
Chas. Green - bp May 8, 1869; dec Feb 25, 1821
Welford Perry - bp May 8, 1869
Orva Perry - bp May 8, 1869; dec
DeLoss Marsh - bp May 8, 1869; rj
Mrs. Chas Woodworth - bp May 8, 1869; dis May 18??
Helen S. Satterlee - bp May 8, 1869; rj
Carrie Campbell Skinner - bp May 8, 1870; d spring of 1913
Geo Campbell - ad 1870; suspended Jan 24, 1874
Martha Lawrence - ad May 27, 1871; dec
Amelia S. Lawrence - ad May 27, 1871; dec
Martha Z. Lawrence - ad May 27, 1871; dec
A.C. Stillman - ad Aug 10, 1872; dis
Dianna Stillman - see above
Amy Lea - bp Feb 1874; dis
Abby Campbell Williams - bp Feb 1874
Anna Mumpton - bp Feb 1874; rj
Edgar Bennett - bp Mar 1874; d Jun 12, 1902
Sarah Bennett - bp Mar 1874; d Apr 27, 1904
Rhoda Williams - bp Mar 1874; dec
Eliza Williams - ad Mar 1874; d 1897
C.M. Lewis - ad Mar 1874; d Feb 17, 1883
Eliza A. Lewis - ad Mar 1874; d Mar 26, 1881
Erlow Lewis - ad Mar 1874; d Apr 30, 1893; 42 yrs
Henry Davis - bp Mar 1874; d Jan 1920
Zillah Warner Showdy - bp Mar 1874
Elizabeth Marsh - bp Mar 1874; d 1885
Mrs. R. W. Davis - bp Mar 1874; rj
Sarah Herreg - bp Mar 1874; dis
Mrs. Jas. Satterlee - bp Mar 1874; dis
Thomas Strobridge - bp Mar 1874; rj
Frank Williams - bp Mar 1874; rj
Geo A. Green - ad Mar 1874; d. Mar 1903
Lovina Green - ad Mar 1874
Geo. Stillman - ad Apr 1874; dis
Nettie Stillman - ad Apr 1874; dis
Joseph Lawton - ad Apr 1874; d Feb 1881
Joanna Lawton - ad Apr 1874; d Dec 10, 1891; 82 yrs
Louisa Witter - ad Aug 8, 1874; d 1918
Sarah Davis w/o D.H. Davis, China missionary - ad Aug 8, 1874; dis
Charles Holcomb - bp Oct 20, 1874; rj 1884

Mary Holcomb - bp Oct 20, 1874; rj Aug 24, 1884
William H. Lewis - bp Oct 20, 1874
Jerimiah Conger - bp Jul 1875; dec
Lilly Williams - bp Jul 24, 1875
Ida Warner Thayer - bp Jul 24, 1775
Henry Pardee - bp Aug 1875; rj
Cora Villiams - bp Aug 1875
Ella Williams Davis - bp Aug 1875; d 1896
Marian Conger - bp Mar 3, 1877; d Sep 2, 1902
Hiram W. Palmiter - bp Mar 3, 1877
J. Lawton Williams - bp Mar, 1877; d 1891
Dea. J. Frank Stilson - bp Mar 24, 1877; d Apr 9, 1896; 55 yrs
Annette Stilson - bp Mar 24, 1877; dec
Margaret Williams - bp May 1877; d Oct 1825
Susan Burdick - bp May 1877; d 1896
Lucinda Williams - bp Apr 1877; d Apr 23, 1893; 85 yrs
Eld. U. M. Babcock - ad 1877; dis
Mrs. U.M. Babcock - ad 1877; dis
John R. Waller - ad Jan 1880; d 1889
Maggie S. Williams w/o Orville - ad Mar 1881; d Jan 26, 1922
Ada E. H. Perry - ad Mar 1881; dec
Susie Stark - bp Apr 1881; d Aug 1995
Nora Perry - bp Apr 1881; dis Feb 4, 1894
Etta Williams - bp Apr 1881; rj Aug 1898
Bertha Marsh Ferguson - bp Apr 1881; dec
Emma Green Herrig - bp Apr 1881
Willie May - bp Apr 1881; dp
Grant Lewis - bp Apr 1881; dp; dec
Annie Conger Davis - ad Apr 1881; dis 1891, 1901
Effie Conger Newey - bp Apr 1881
Mrytie Conger Williams - bp Apr 1881; d 1955
Abbie R. Lewis - ad Dec 31, 1881; dis Mar 11, 1882
Rev. Hermon D. Clark - ad Nov 1, 1883; dis
Daniel C. Starkey - bp Jun 28, 1885; NR; dis
Eld. J. E. N. Backus - ad Apr 9, 1887; d Feb 24, 1899
Mrs. J.E. N. Backus - ad Apr 9, 1887; NR; dis
Sarah Backus - bp Apr 9, 1887; dp 1899
A.A. Thayer - bp 1888
Alfred B. H. Backus - bp Jun 8, 1889; dis Dec 1891
Mrs. Lois M. Newey - bp Jun 1889; d Mar 7, 1914
Jennie M. Newey - bp Jun 1889; d Nov 15, 1894; 18 yrs
Vic J. Newey Warner - bp Jun 1889
Emily Batson - (written in later, no information)
Emma M. Conger - bp Jun 1889
Flora M. Williams Hyde Davis - bp Jun 1885; d May 1947
M. Lucille Stark - Jun 1885; d Ap 21, 1895
Josephine Lewis - bp Jun 1885; rj Aug 16, 1898
Henrietta Lewis - bp Jun 1885; rj Aug 16, 1898
Rev. Henry L. Jones - ad May 6, 1891; dis Feb 24, 1894
Emma Jones - see above
Blanche Newey Williams - bp Jun 1892
Ira A. Newey - bp Jun 1892
Cally Palmiter Smith - bp Jun 1892
Edith Thayer Woodcock - bp Jun 1892

Charles Mills - bp Jun 1892
Orley H. Perry - bp Jun 1892; dis
Erving Williams - bp Jun 1892
Henry Warner - bp Jun 1892
Eld. Joshua Clark - ad Feb 24, 1894; d Feb 9, 1895; 73 yrs
Sister J. Clark - ad Feb 24, 1894; d 1910
O. J. Davis - ad Mar 3, 1894; dis Aug 1901; reinstated Jul 14, 1906
Annie Davis - see above
W. D. Hyde - ad Mar 31, 1894; d Mar 1900
R. Cora Davis Keller - ad Aug 4, 1895
Emily E. Davis Thorngate - ad Aug 4, 1895
Pastor Martin Sindall - ad Sep 1895; dis
Cora B. Sindall - see above entry
Joseph Burdick - bp May 1896; d 1898
George Williams - bp May 1896; d 1900
Lualla Perry Bennett - bp May 1896
Lela Palmiter Franklin - bp May 1896
Alex Rhodes - bp Aug 1, 1896; d 1920
Lydia Rhodes - bp Aug 1, 1896
Celestia Davis - ad May 22, 1897; d 1911
Sylvester White - bp May 14, 1898; dec
William Moore Sr - bp May 14, 1898; dec
Mrs. William Moore Sr - bp May 14, 1898; d Dec 9, 1905
Milford Decker - bp May 14, 1898; dp Jan 10, 1910
Mrs. Milford Decker - bp May 14, 1898
Mable Decker Webb - bp May 14, 1898; dec
Pausy Decker Webb - bp May 14, 1898; dec
Ira Rhodes - May 14, 1898; dp Aug 4, 1900
Mrs. Charles Rounds - bp May 14, 1898
C. N. Rounds - bp May 14, 1898
Rev. G. V. Lewis - ad Sep 23, 1899; dis Sep 1901
Ella J. Lewis w/o G.V. - see above entry
Miss Sarah Boardman - bp Sep 22, 1900; dp
Sarah Williams Lowe - bp Sep 22, 1900
George Betson - ad Sep 14, 1901; dis or dp Sep 14, 1901
Rev. Leon D. Burdick - ad 1902; dp Jan 15, 1905
Rev. Pierre R. Burdick - ad 1902; dp Mar 4, 1905
Genivieve Burdick - bp 1902; dis Mar 4, 1905
Lois A. Newey Stone - bp 1902
Rev. A. L. Davis - ad 1902; dis
Mrs. A. L. Davis - ad 1902; dis
Mable Perry - ad 1902; dis
Zilla Thayer - bp Jul 7, 1906
Cerena Davis - bp 1906; dis
Merril Davis - bp 1906
Eva Rhoades Perkins - bp 1906
Ovville Hyde - bp 1906
Mildred Warner Lennon - bp 1906
O. J. Davis - reinstated Jul 14, 1906; dis
Mrs. O. J. Davis - see above entry
Henry Pradee - restored Jun 30, 1907; dp Jan 19, 1916
Grace Decker - bp Jul 7, 1907; dp Jan 10, 1910
Lamont Stillman - ad May 30, 1908;   dis
Mrs. Lamont Stillman - see above entry

Guy H. Davis - bp May 30, 1908
Ceril Davis - bp May 30, 1908
Stuart Smith - bp May 30, 1908; dec
Mrs. Mary Prentice - ad Mayy 30, 1908; d Nov 1913
Artheda Hyde Langworthy - bp Oct 2, 1909; dec
Genevieve Hyde - bp Oct 2, 1909
Clarence Davis - bp Apr 9, 1910
Allen Lennon - bp Apr 9, 1910
Allen Davis - bp Apr 9, 1910; dis
Eula Warner Sholtz - bp Apr 9, 1910
Marian Edwin Dillman - bp Oct 7, 1911
Chester Stone - bp Jun 8, 1912
Rev. R. R. Thorngate - ad Jul 6, 1912
Mrs. Zilla D. Thorngate - ad Jul 6, 1912; d Mar 1914
Roscoe M. Thorngate - ad Jul 12, 1912; dp
Julia B. Thorngate - ad Jul 12, 1912; dis
Mrs. Rachil David - ad Jul 12, 1912; dec
Beatrice W. Thayer - bp Aug 16, 1913
Alice Dillman Hyde - bp Aug 16, 1913
Ivamore Perry Williams - bp Jun 2, 1912
Eld. William Simpson - ad Aug 5, 1916; dis
Mrs. Amelia Simpson - see above entry
Nelson Hunt - ad 1916 by testimony
Lavern Davis - bp 1916
Mrs. Dea Mills - ad 1916 by testimony
Bertha Williams - bp 1917
Marion C. W. Sholtz - bp 1917
Jennie M. W. Sholtz - 1917
Effie M. Burdick Jones - bp 1916
Stanley Warner - bp 1916
Mary Williams - ad Oct 27, 1917
Earl Williams - ad Oct 27, 1917
Millicent Stuckey Williams - ad Oct 27, 1917
J. M. Sholtz - ad Aug 10, 1918
Mrs. Effie Sholtz - ad Aug 19, 1918

REVISED LIST OF FIRST VERONA   1922

Mary Gardner Allen - bp Feb 26, 1853; d Mar 1, 1926
Caroline S. Green Stark -   ad Jul 1, 1855; d Oct 13, 1923
Flora E. Green Palmiter - bp Mar 28, 1868; d Jan 20, 1924
Welford C. Perry - bp May 8, 1869
Abbie Campbell Williams - bp Feb 1874; d Dec 15, 1934
Zilla Warner Showdy - bp Mar 1874; Dec 27, 1932
Lovinia Green - ad Mar 1874; d Dec 19, 1923
William H. Lewis - bp Oct 20, 1874; d Oct 1938
Lillian Williams - bp Jul 24, 1875; d Oct 1938
Ida Warner Thayer - bp Jul 24, 1875;
Dea. Hiram W. Palmiter - bp Mar 17, 1877; d Jan 23, 1923
Frank H. Williams - bp Mar 17, 1877; d Feb 19, 1926
Timmie Williams - bp Mar 17, 1877
Annette M. Stilson - bp Mar 24, 1877; d Jul 4, 1925
Margaret Williams - bp May 1896. d Oct 29, 1925

Susie B. Stark - bp Apr 1881; d Aug 1955
Emma Green Herrig - bp Apr 1881; d Feb 3, 1924
Effie Conger Newey - bp Apr 1881
Myrtie Conger Williams - Apr 1881; d 1955
Arthur A. Thayer - bp 1888; d Oct 10, 1924
Vil Newey Warner - bp Jun 1889
Emily Conger Betson - bp Jun 1889; dis
Flora Williams Hyde Davis - bp Jun 1889
Blanche Newey Williams - bp Jun 1892
Dea. Ira A. Newey - bp Jun 1892
Grace Green - bp Jun 1892
Carrie Palmiter Smith - bp Jun 1892
Edith Thayer Woodcock - bp Jun 1892
Chas. Mills - bp Jun 1892
Orlo H. Perry - bp Jun 1892
Irving J. Williams - bp Jun 1892
Henry B. Warner - bp Jun 1892; d Aug 1936
R. Cora Davis Keller - bp Aug 4, 1895; d 1942
Emily E. Davis Thorngate - bp Aug 4, 1895; dis Sep 3, 1927
Lualta Perry Bennet - bp May 16, 1896
Leila Palmiter Franklin - bp May 16, 1896
Mrs. Lydia Rhoades - bp Aug 1, 1896; d 1937
Mrs. Milford Decker - bp May 14, 1898
Sarah Williams Lowe - bp Sep 22, 1900
Geo. W. Betson - ad Sep 14, 1901; dis
Lois Newey Stone - bp 1902
Mable Perry - bp 1902
Zilla Thayer Vierow - bp Jul 7, 1906
Eva Rhoades Taylor - bp Jul 7, 1906; dp Feb 2, 1929
Orville W. Hyde - bp Jul 7, 1906; d Nov 17, 1973
Mildred Warner Lennin - bp Jul 7, 1906
Guy Howard Davis - bp May 30, 1908; dec
T. Stuart Smith - bp May 30, 1908; dec
Artheda Hyde Langworthy - bp Oct 2, 1909; dis Oct 6, 1923
Geneieve Hyde Stone - bp Oct 2, 1909
Allen Lennon bp Aug 20, 1910
Eula Warner Sholtz - bp Aug 20, 1910
Marion E. Dillman - bp Oct 7, 1911
Chester Stone - bp Jun 8, 1912
Beatrice Williams Thayer - bp Aug 16, 1913
Alice Dillman Hyde - Aug 16, 1913
Ivanore Perry Dillman - Jun 8, 1912
Nelson Hunt - ad Aug 5, 1919 by testimony; d Aug 6, 1929
La Verne W. Davis - bp 1916
Mrs. Emma Mills - ad 1916 by testimony; d Jan 9, 1930
Effie Burdick Jones - bp 1916; dp Apr 6, 1929
Stanley Warner - bp 1916; d Jun 15, 1973
Bertha Williams - bp 1917; dp Mar 25, 1932
Marion C. Williams Sholtz - bp 1917
Jennie M. Williams Sholtz - bp 1917; d Jan 10, 1975
Millicent Stukey Williams - ad Oct 27, 1917
Mary Whitford Williams - ad Oct 27, 1917
Earl Williams - ad Oct 27, 1917d Dec 27, 1924
Joseph M. Sholtz - ad Aug 10, 1918; d Jan 12, 1944

Mrs. Effie Davis Sholtz; ad Aug 10, 1918; d Jun 23, 1930
Craig Sholtz - ad Aug 10, 1918
Raymond Sholtz - ad Aug 10, 1918
Claude Sholtz - ad Aug 10, 1918
Floyd Sholtz - ad Aug 10, 1918
Ruth Sholtz Davis - ad Aug 10, 1910
Eld T. J. Van Horn - ad 1919; dis 1925
Mrs. Harriet C. Van Horn - ad 1919
Iris Sholtz Maltby - bp Sep 1919
Iva M. Davis - ad Sep 1919
Orlo H. Perry - ad Mar 1920
Mable L. Perry - ad Mar 1920
John W. Williams - ad Mar 1920
Alfred L. Perry - bp Mar 22, 1920
James Ameyden - ad May 22, 1920; dis Dec 13, 1930
Mrs. Nellie Ameyden - ad May 22, 1920; dis Dec 13, 1930
Henry Ameyden - bp May 22, 1920; dis Dec 13, 1930
Hendrina Ameyden - bp May 22, 1920; dis Dec 13, 1930
Chester Williams - bp May 22, 1920
Rosalind Williams - bp May 22, 1920
Lola Woodcock Getman - bp May 22, 1920
Horatio S. West - ad May 22, 1920 by testimony; d Apr 7, 1923
Mrs. Emily Joslin West - bp May 22, 1920 by testimony; d 1938
Arthur G. Newey - bp Jan 9, 1921; d Feb 12, 1927
Thos. C. Davis - ad Jul 16, 1921; d Apr 24, 1932
Eudora Perry Green - bp Oct 1, 1921
Sylvia Babcock Carr - ad May 27, 1922
Ruby Davis - ad May 27, 1922; d Oct 19, 1929
Flora Smith Babcock - bp Aug 5, 1922; dis
Agnes Smith Marquandt - bp Aug 5, 1922
Anna Smith Davis - bp Aug 5, 1922; dis 1953-4
Harriet Franklin Davis - bp Aug 5, 1922
Ethel Keller Filey - bp Aug 5, 1922
Marjory Stone Beaver - bp Aug 5, 1922
Bernice Lennon Fargo - bp Aug 5, 1922
Jean Woodcock Lyng - bp Aug 5, 1922
Elmina C. Warner - ad Aug 5, 1922
Grace Decker Miller - ad Jan 10, 1924 reinstated
Mrs. Florence Stukey - ad Jul 5, 1924 by testimony
Ada Dillman - bp Jun 14, 1924
Dena Ameyden - bp Jun 14, 1924; dis Dec 13, 1930
Leslie Miller - bp Jun 14, 1924
Harold Miller - bp Jun 14, 1924
Roger Lennon - bp Jun 14, 1924
William Lennon - bp Jun 14, 1924
Rev. Jas. Hurley - ad May 2, 1925; dis Apr 25, 1926
Mrs. Jas. H. Hurley - see above entry
Jesse L. Williams - ad Feb 6, 1926; d 1938
James Ameyden Jr - bp Apr 24, 1926; dis Dec 13, 1930
Pastor Lester G. Osborn - ad May 15, 1926; dis Oct 1, 1932
Mrs. Grace Osborn - see above entry
Gladys M. Hyde Tracy - bp Jul 30, 1927
Gertrude F. Hyde - bp Jul 30, 1927
Viola Chaplin Van Dresen - ad Aug 6, 1927 by testimomy

Frances Babcock Sholtz - ad Nov 6, 1927
Gladys Hillman - Apr 26, 1930
June West - bp Apr 26, 1930
Madeline West - bp Apr 26, 1930
Alta Dillman - bp Apr 26, 1930
G. Allison Smith - bp Apr 26, 1930
Orville A. Williams - Apr 26, 1930
Charles Chaplin - Apr 26, 1930
John Byrnes - Apr 26, 1930
Mrs. Elizabeth Revely Smith - bp Apr 26, 1930; d Dec 1935
Alice West Chaplin - ad Apr 26, 1930 by testimony
Arminta West Byrner - ad Apr 26, 1930 by testimony
A. Warner Thayer - ad Apr 26, 1930 by testimony
Pastor George Sorensen - ad Jul 12, 1930; d Dec 15, 1931
Mrs. Louise Sorensen - see above entry
Eula E. Lennon - bp Jul 16, 1932
Walter Davis - bp Jul 16, 1932
Rev. A. L. Davis - ad Jul 16, 1932
Mrs. Flora Davis - ad Jul 16, 1932
George Davis - ad Jul 16, 1932; dis 1953-4
Alfred Davis - ad Jul 16, 1932
Geraldine Thorngate - ad Nov 5, 1932 by testimony
Gerald Tracy - bp Nov 5, 1932; dp
Mrs. Gertrude Deely - Aug 4, 1934 by testimony
Miss Jennie Bird - bp Aug 11, 1934
Alva Warner - bp Jan 1935
Garth Warner - bp Jan 1935
Warren Stone - bp Jan 1935
Alden Vierow - bp Jan 1935
Helen Davis - bp Jan 1935
Anita Dillman - bp Jan 1935
Milford Decker - Jun 6, 1936 reunited; d Aug 136
Dorothy Williams - bp 1939
Doris Lennen
Olin Davis
David Williams
Ralph M. Sopher

CRR 1980.8.3   vault
First Verona, NY Church Records 1841-1932
IMS:1993

SECOND VERONA 1864-1903
State Bridge, Oneida Co, NY

Eld. Halsey Stillman - ad Mar 6, 1869
Pamela Stillman - ad Mar 6, 1869
Lilly Stillman - bp May 22, 1889
Ida Stillman - bp May 22, 1889
Mary F. Reynolds - ad Aug 30, 1873
Emma L. Mills - bp Aug 30, 1873
Eld. Alex Campbell - ad Aug 30, 1873
Leilly West - bp Jul 17, 1875
Clarinda Campbell- ad Aug 30, 1873
John Satterly - bp Jul 31, 1875
George W. Burdick - bp Jul 24, 1875
Mrs. Fanny West - bp Jul 31, 75
Charles Satterlee - bp Jul 17, 1875
Clara Satterlee - bp Aug 21, 75
Catharine Satterlee - bp Jul 17, 1875; dis
Frederick E. Wolfe - bp Jul 24, 1875
Julia Satterlee - bp Aug 21, 75
David H. King - bp Aug 21, 1875; dis Sep 5, 1875
Joseph V. Parmilee - bp Aug 21, 1875
Helen Parmilee - bp Aug 21, 75
Zacheus T. Burdick - ad Aug 28, 1875
Adell West - bp 1884
Sarah Lovina Burdick - ad Aug 28, 1875 by statement
Laodicia Satterlee - bp Aug Aug 5, 1876
Haratio S. West - bp 1884
Thelma Satterlee - bp 1884
Curtis Hunt - Aug 10, 1889
Alice Hunt - bp 1884
Elinor Burdick - ad Jul 30, 1887

MS 1984.25.1
CRR   NY state box   vault
State Bridge Membershipship List 1869-1899 detached
IMS: 1993

SECOND VERONA SDB Society Sep 2, 1875

List of People Contributing to Repair of Church Building

Dea. Joseph West - $50
George T. Hunt - $20
Francis Mills
R. W. West
Zacheus T. Burdick
Joseph V. Pamalee
Joseph A. West
Sporing Monroe $25
William E. Vitter $50
Orville Williams $2
Alvin Lawrence $5
Nelson R. Satterlee $10
William Davis $10
Chris Beck $2
James Newton $1
Henry White $5
Anderson Walker $5
George A. Campbell $5
William Davis $10
D. H. Davis $15
Ira Green $5
William H. Lewis $1
Orville Williams $2
William S. Potter $20
D. B. Fay $2
Archible Hess
Alvin F. Lawrence
J. C. Felter
S. H. Bortle
George M. White
William Crandall
James Newton
Mathias Smith

William E. Vitter - $50.
George H. Satterlee - $20
Nelson R. Satterlee
Edwin P. Satterlee
Fred E. Wolf
G. A. Campbell
George Satterlee $20
Archible Hess $25
Eld. D. H. Davis $15
D. B. Hay $2
John C. Felter $5
Ira Green $5
William Crandall $2
Richard Stone $1
F. H. Williams $1
George White $5
Oscar Williams $5
Frank Reynolds $5
Christ Beck
William Williams
R. W. Davis
Orin Williams
Oscar Williams
C. B. Stark
Geo A. Campbell $ 5
John Shively
F. H. Williams
Sporing Monroe
Henry White
Andrew Walker
Richard Stone
Andrew Duskee
Anson Palms

CRR 1984.25.2 NY state box vault
2nd Verona Society Records 1845-1901

IMS: 1993

SYRACUSE NY SDB Church Records   1909-1965

Members

Leon E. Cross - ad Jan 23, 1909
Edith S. Cross - ad Jan 23, 1909
Herman J. Cross - ad Jan 23, 1909; d Jul 27, 1945
Clara L. Cross - ad Jul 23, 1909; d Mar 9, 1954
Nancy A. Parslow - ad Jan 23, 1909; d Sep 17, 1910
Marion A. Parslow - ad Jan 23, 1909; d Mar 1962
Jennie M. Broderick - ad Jan 23, 1909; d Apr 25, 1958
    Mrs. Seamans - RD 3 Cortland NY; 121 Dewey Ave, Fayetteville NY
Mrs. Mary A. Broderick Batson - ad Jan 23, 1909;
    c/o Mark Broderick - Roaring Branch PA; 314 E. 28 St., Balt. MD
Mabel E. Parslow - ad Jan 23, 1909; d Jun 17, 1912
Geogianna C. Cross Wilmot - ad Jan 23, 1909; d Sep 29, 1909
George L. Wilmot - ad Jan 23, 1909; Los Angeles CA
George W. Cross - ad Apr 1909; d Feb 11, 1913
Edna M. Stillman - ad Jan 23, 1909; dis Apr 26, 1919
Edwin S. Maxson - ad Jan 23, 1909; d (?) Oct 21, 1933
Laydia L. Bush - ad Oct 13, 1909; d Mar 28, 1918
Celestia M. Davis - Ad Oct 16, 1909; d May 23, 1911
Emoline B. White - ad Oct 15, 1910; d 1928
    Mrs. Helen White: c/o Benton C. White, Sidney NY
Bertha W. Bly - ad Oct 15, 1910; Tangaco PA
Irving Charles Bly - ad Dec 17, 1910
Edwin Maxson Cross - ad Dec 17, 1910
Riley G. Davis - ad Jul 8, 1911; dead
Viola H. Davis - ad Jul 8, 1911; dead
Fornia Wallace Davis - ad Jan 24, 1914; (W.VA)
    believed to have joined Salvation Army
Helen C. Roe - ad May 2, 1914; dead
J. Harold Roe - ad Jan 29, 1916
Elizabeth M. Monroe - ad Jan 29, 1916; d 1930
Mabel L. Perry - ad Jan 29, 1916
Orlo H. Perry - ad Jan 29, 1916
William Clayton - ad Feb 19, 1916; d Dec 23, 1931
Frances Clayton - ad Mar 24, 1917; d Mar 1929
John Claxton Forgar - ad May 26, 1917
Ida B. Forgar - ad May 26, 1917
Charkes B. Forgar - ad May 26, 1917; joned Salvation Army
Charles Irving Cross - ad Mar 22, 1919
Harriette Marie Cross - ad Mar 22, 1919
Charles Molau Kingman - bp Mar 15, 1924
Gertrude Case Smith - ad Mar 15, 1924; d May 21, 1943
Lars Peter Jensen - ad Aug 29, 1925
Mrs Edna R. Baldwin - transferred to Leonardsville
Robert Clinton Spaid - ad 1937
Dorothy Claire Spaid - (D. F. Whitcomb) ad 1937
John E. Tily - ad Sep 1941
Leon R. Tily - ad Sep 13, 1941
Sally Jane Tily - bp Aug 19, 1950
William Alfred Tily - ad Aug 5, 1950
Sue Tily - ad Sep 1955

Marion M. Brannon - ad May 22, 1965
Arline S. Burdick - ad May 22, 1965
Wayne Burdick - ad May 22, 1965
Larry G. Brannon - ad May 22, 1965
Nancy R. Brannon - ad May 22, 1965
Warren F. Brannon - ad May 22, 1965
James Van Ameyden - ad May 5, 1965; d May 13, 1966
Marrion Whipple w/o Henry - ad Dec 3, 1966
Henry Whipple - ad Dec 3, 1966
Esther Burdick - ad associate member Dec 3, 1966; full at Verona
Nancy Cruzan - ad associate member Dec 3, 1966; full at Milton
Rev. Ralph Hays - ad associate member Feb 11, 1067; full at Adams Center
Mary Hays w/o Ralph - see above entry
Sally Hays - see above entry
Ralph Hays, Jr. - see above entry
Nancy Burdick - associate member Dec 16, 1967; full at Berlin

CRR 1970.12   New York state box   vault
Syracuse NY SDB Church Records 1909-1965
IMS:1993

ADAMS CENTER 1822–
Jefferson Co. NY

Chas Greene s/o Waite Bailey & Charles - ad June 9, 1822
    b Oct 10, 1778, d May 9, 1878
Mary (Polly) Greene Potter Green w/o Clarke Greene,d/o Waite Bailey &
    Chas, wid/o Daniel Potter -   ad Oct 27. 1824; b Apr 20, 1775
Mary Crosby prob. w/o Ransom Coon - ad May 14, 1824, d Nov 12, 1890
Adonis Trowbridge - ad May 1, 1830; d Dec 2, 1880
Mrs. Adonis Trowbridge (Fanny) - ad June 5, 1830; d May 20, 1882
Eliza Greene Dewey w/o Joel - d/o Amy Sheldon & Chas
    ad May 1, 1830; b. Nov 30, 1809, d Oct 24, 1835
Lucy Lee Babcock w/o Nelson - ad June 5, 1830; d Nov 18, 1881
Celia Amy Greene Washburn w/o Freeman - d/o Amy Sheldon & Chas
    ad Apr 19, 1833; b Dec 8, 1818, d May 30, 1896
Clarissa Benjamin Babcock w/o Pardon - ad Apr 19, 1833
Marg't Whitford Maxson w/o Silas - d/o Polly Maxson & Maj. Ed
    ad Nov 25, 1836; d Dec 6, 1888
Almyra Burdick Babcock w/o Samuel - mother of Malone
    ad May 3, 1837, d Nov 13, 1883
Sophie White fr Brookfield - ad May 6, 1837; d Nov 18, 1884
Chas Potter s/o Mary Stillman & Capt. George - ad Sep 1'37, d May 30'82
Eliza Burdick Potter w/o Chas - d/o Pollie Stillman & Sam'l
    ad Sep 1, 1837, d June 3, 1877
Matilda Saunders - ad Sep 1, 1837; d Nov 17, 1884
Dr. Edwin R. Maxson - ad Jan 6, 1838; d Jan 25, 1812
Leonard R. Greene s/o Betsey Kenyon & Jos. - ad Jan 6, 1838
    b July 22, 1820, d May 2, 1907
Jas. G. s/o Mary Gavitt & Jas. J. Greene (Petersburg Josie)
    ad Jan 6, 1838; b Feb 14, 1818, d Aug 6, 1898
Mary Ann Clark Greene wid/Larry Greeene - w/o J. Reeves - d/o Jemima
    Sturervant & Josh; ad Jan 6, 1838, b Mar 25, 1828, d Feb 1893
Paul Jr s/o Nancy Gardner & Paul Greene - ad Jan 27, 1838
    b Mar 16, 1808, d Dec 19, 1894
Almira Burdick Greene w/o Jas. A. - d/o Sally Bell & Bela
    ad Jan 27, 1838, b July 21, 1821
Waite Greene Ford w/o Ebenezer - d/o Hannah Nichols & Uncle Josie
    ad Feb 15, 1840, d Mar 26, 1878
Margaret Sweet Hull w/o Frank - d/o Anna Greene & Ira
    ad Apr 18, 1840, b 1832, d May 6, 1898

p. 2
Phebe Otis Greene w/o Truman - d/o Thankful Heath & William
    ad Sep 23, 1840, b Jan 11, 1811, d Nov 4, 1877
Lorenzo Greene s/o Mercy Chase & Ethan - ad Dec 10, 1840
    b Sep 7, 1805, d Aug 15, 1877
Palmer s/o Nancy Gardner & Paul Greene - ad Mar 5, 1842
    b Jan 3, 1814, d Feb 5, 1889
John Reeve s/o Nancy Gardner & Paul Greene - ad Mar 5, 1842
    b July 2, 1822, d 1898
Laura Greene Potter w/o Samuel - d/o Nancy Gardner & Paul
    ad Mar 5, 1842, b Apr 2, 1823, d Aug 16, 1890

Orilla Jones Greene w/o Lorenzo - d/o Betsey Randell & William
    ad Mar 20, 1842 , b Dec 18, 1812, d Feb 18, 1882
Polly d/o Mercy Chase & Ethan Greene - ad May 28, 1842
    b Feb 25, 1817, d Nov 11, 1897
Dr. Correl D. Potter s/o Eliza Burdick & Chas
    ad Apr 5, 1845, d Feb 28, 1893
Britta Maxson d/o Betsey Brown & Jesse; ad Apr 5, 1845, d Oct 1893
Esther Maxson Millard w/o George - Betsey Brown & Jesse
    ad Oct 5, 1845, Oct 19, 1889
Dea. Nathan G. Whitford s/o Olive Burdick & Jesse
    ad May 4, 1845, d Oct 10, 1911
Charlotte Sheath Whitford w/o Nathan - d/o Dorcas Rarhbone & Jacob
    ad May 4, 1845, d July 1902
Ann Eliza Bliss Wakefield - teacher Greene settlement; ad June 29, 1849
Dorleska Armsbury Coon w/o Jos. - d/o George; ad Jun 29'45, d Jun 13, 1900
Paul Potter s/o Esther Greene & Silas - ad Oct 18, 1845
    b. 1827, d Apr 11, 1881
Leander R. Greene - youngest s/o Amy Sheldon & Chas.; ad Oct 18, 1845
    b Oct 12, 1929, d Apr 15, 1915
Lucinda Potter Wood w/o George - d/o Esther Greene & Silas
    ad Oct 18, 1845, b Mar 13, 1845, d Jun 16, 1901
Jenette Greene Gibbs w/o B.F. - d/o Nancy Gardner & Paul
    ad Oct 18, 1845, May 30, 1896
Dorcas Greene - ad Oct 18, 1845
Cinderella Greene Bates w/o Samuel Alva - youngest child of Amy
    Sheldon & Chas.; ad Oct 18, 1845, b June 19, 1833, d June 1, 1926
Franklin J. Greene s/o Mary Gavit & Jos. J.; ad Oct 25, 1845
    b Apr 27, 1822, d. Mar 17, 1897
Samuel M. Potter s/o Hannah Niles & Chas. G. - ad Oct 25, 1845
    b Mar 27, 1822, d Sep 6, 1879
Silas Maxson s/o Dea. Hollyof Scott (?) - ad Oct 31, 1845, d Apr 15'88
Phila Trowbridge Woodward w/o Constant - d/o Adonis & Fanny
    ad Dec 26, 1846, Dec 1, 1825, age 90

p. 3
Lucy Lanphier Maxson w/o Dr. Edwin R. - d/o Samuel & Hannah
    ad July 3, 1847, d Feb 24, 1910
Lemon De Esting Greene s/o Ann Sweet & Thos. H.
    ad Mar 4, 1848, b Nov 4, 1833, d Sep 11, 1920 at Bath
William M. Greene s/o Eliza Williams & Mathew - ad Mar 4, 1848
    b May 4, 1834, d Jan 17, 1894
Delia Potter Gardner w/o George - d/o Eliza Burdick & Chas
    ad Mar 4, 1848, d Jul 9, 1907
Thompson W. Saunders - ad Apr 29, 1848, d Jan 27, 1895
Susan Armsbury Saunders w/o Thompson - prob d/o George of Petersburo
    ad Apr 30, 1848, d Oct 1884
Sally Ann Whitford Greene w/o Spicer Greene - wid/o Barton Whitford
    sister Rev. Halsey Baker; ad Jun 17, 1848, d Apr 3, 1897
Zebulon J. Scrivens s/o Cath Greene & Dan'l - ad June 20, 1850
    b Nov 11, 1836, d May 1893
Andrew J. s/o Clarissa White & Butch Josie G. - ad June 20, 1850
    b Dec 15, 1832, d Sep 13, 1916
Mary Adelia Scrivens Greene w/o Leander - d/o Cath & Dan'l
    ad Jun 20, 1850, b Aug 27, 1832, d Aug 20, 1909

Abigail Saunders Jones w/o Phelander - d/o Ann Budlong & Roswell
    ad June 20, 1850, d Oct 7, 1914
Mary Hull Greene w/o Andrew J. - d/o Prudence Whitford & Jos.
    ad June 20, 1850, b Jan 31, 1832, d Oct 6, 1889
M. Antoinette Greene Clark w/o Edwin - eldest child Hannah Jones &
    Paul Jr.; ad June 20, 1850, b May 4, 1932 d Jan 13, 1885
P. Melissa Greene Greene w/o O. DeGrass - second child Hannah Jones &
    Paul Jr; ad June 20, 1850, b Nov 28, 1833, d June 3, 1900
M. Satira Greene Coon w/o Chas; 4th child Hannah Jones & Paul Jr
    ad June 20, 1850, b May 12, 1837, d Aug 12, 1905
Augusta Greene Gurley w/o Harrison D. - d/o Harriet Maxson &
    Spicer; ad June 20, 1850, b Feb 28, 1837, d Mar 13, 1893
Susan J. Greene Brundedge eldest d/o Harriet Maxson & Spicer
    ad June 20, 1850, b Feb 9, 1835, d June 7, 1905
Edwin Clark s/o Jermima Sturtevant & Josh. - ad Jul 1850, d July 29, 1908
Philander Jones s/o Betsey Randell & William - ad July 1850, d Sep 30'90
Spicer Greene s/o Mary Gavit & Jos. J. (Petersburg Josie)
    ad Jan 4, 1852, b Oct 19, 1806, d Sep 19, 1887
Lucretia Babcock Crosby w/o E. Curtis - d/o Lucy Lee & Nelson
    ad Feb 7, 1852, d July 7, 1906
Angenette Maxson Kellog 2nd w/o Isaac - d/o Jesse; ad Feb 7, 1852
    d Sep 4, 1916
Angeline Babcock d/o Almira Burdick & Samuel - ad Feb 7, 1852
Orange DeGrass Greene s/o Ann Sweet & Thos. H. - ad Feb 21, 1852
    b June 19, 1831, d Mar 14, 1911
Juliette Hull Crosby w/o Henry - d/o Prudence Whitford & Jos.
    ad Feb 21, 1852, d July 31, 1902
Rosanna Greene Gurley w/o David - d/o Amy Sheldon & Chas.
    ad Mar 5, 1852, b May 11, 1820, d May 11, 1877

p. 4
Alvah G. Greene s/o Susannah Williams & Caleb G. - ad May 2, 1852
    d May 4, 1803, d Nov 20, 1885
Dea. Edwd D. Spicer s/o Content Potter & Jos. - ad May 6'52, Ex Nov 2'79
Eliza Wells Spicer w/o Edward - d/o Sophia Stillman & Geo.
    ad May 6, 1852, d June 6, 1878
Zadock Clark s/o Jemima Sturtevant & Josh - ad Aug 13, 1852; EX
Eleanor Greene d/o Orilla Jones & Lorenzo - ad Nov 5, 1852
    b May 10, 1834, d Feb 4, 1907
Emeline Davis Green w/o Palmer Sr - d/o Amelia Jones & William
    ad Oct 1854, b July 17, 1816, d Feb 3, 1880
Eliza A. Greene Quible d/o Betsey Kenyon & Jos.
    b July 19, 1815, d Feb 13, 1901
Rev. William G. Quible pastor husband of Eliza - ad Nov 2, 1855
    d Jan 1, 1885, age 79
Sarah Gardner w/o Job - d/o Adonis & Fanny Trowbridge
    ad Sep 1, 1855, d Dec 21, 1898
Geo. Wash. Greene s/o Nancy Gardner & Paul G. - ad Feb 16, 1856
    b Dec 23, 1827, d Nov 23, 1916
M. De Chois Greene s/o Hannah Jones & Paul Jr - ad Feb 16, 1856
    b Feb 2, 1839, d Dec 27, 1876
Harrison D. Gurley s/o Rosannah Greene & David - ad Feb 16, 1856
    b Dec 29, 1840, d July 13, 1919

Henry H. Crosby s/o Lucretia Greene & Samuel - ad Feb 16, 1856
    b Jan 10, 1836, d Jan 21, 1881
William DeFrance Greene s/o Hannah Jones & Paul Jr - ad Feb 16, 1856
    b Jan 2, 1841, d May 31, 1911
Albert O. H. Whitford s/o Charlotte Heath & Nathan - ad Feb 16, 1856
    b Dec 17, 1842, d Nov 23, 1912
Dea. George W. Wood - ad Feb 16, 1856, d Feb 10, 1901
Orville G. Green s/o Harriet Maxson & Spicer - ad Feb 16, 1856
    b Nov 23, 1842, d Feb 19, 1927
Dea. Gould Trowbridge s/o Adonis & Fanny Trowbridge
    ad Feb 16, 1856 d Jul 11, 1903
Andrew S. Heath s/o Anna Green Sweet & Elias - ad Feb 16, 1856
    b May 29, 1840, d May 8, 1908
Mary J. Greene Potter w/o Bailey - ad Feb 16, 1856, d Apr 7, 1916
Lucy Greene Crandall d/o Orilla Jones & Lorenzo - ad Feb 16, 1856
    b June 7, 1840, dis to N. Loup NB Jul 4, 1891
Alzina K. Crosby Glass w/o Albert G. - d/o Lucretia Greene & Samuel
    ad Feb 16, 1856, b Sep 15, 1843, d May 26, 1898
Amy Gould Maxson w/o Stillman - d/o Sophronia LeValley & Ora
    ad Feb 16, 1856, d Sep 18, 1814
Anna Marie Whitford w/o Manning Freeman - d/o Sally Ann Green &
    Dea. Edwd Whitford - ad Feb 16, 1856, b Aug 1, 1839, dis 1862
Amelia L. Babcock Greene 1st w/o Thos R. - d/o Lucy Lee & Nelson
    ad Feb 16, 1856, d Jan 24, 1891
Peregrin Douglas came from Altmar - ad Feb 23, 1856, d Oct 28, 1891
Elizabeth Douglas w/o Peregrin - ad Feb 13, 1856, d Sep 18, 1901

p. 5
Bailey Potter s/o Esther Greene & Sias G. - ad Mar 1, 1856
    b Feb 18, 1832, d Mar, 1885
Dan'l A. Greene s/o Amelia Babcock & Thos R. - ad Mar 1'56, d Oct 23'09
Willis A. Babcock s/o Lucy Lee & Nelson - ad Mar 1, 1856, d Dec 10, 1917
Henrietta Foster Potter - ad Mar 1, 1856, (can't trace)d May 17, 1776
Ursula Maxson Chase w/o Henry C. - d/o Roxy Greene & Samuel P.
    ad Mar 1, 1856, b July 24, 1840, Oct 25, 1911
Josephine Maxson Greene w/o Quincy DeForest - Marg't Whitford & Silas
    ad Mar 1, 1856, b June 10, 1824, d June 5, 1907
Madora Maxson Greene 1st w/o DeFrance - d/o Marg't Whitford & Silas
    ad Mar 1, 1856, b July 27, 1843, d July 11, 1884
Electa Ayars Potter w/o C.D. - ad Mar 1, 1856, d Jan 19, 1914
Lenche L. Greene Heath w/o Jas C. - d/o Eliza Williams & Matt.
    ad Mar 1, 1856, b June 4, 1843, d Nov 15, 1915
John Greene Coon s/o Sarah Greene & Dea. Asa Coon
    ad Mar 22, 1856, b Aug 24, 1817, d Dec 4, 1889
Dorcas Vars Coon w/o John Green - ad Mar 22, 1856, d Aug 20, 1917
Malora M. Washburn w/o Chas Lewis - d/o Celia Greene & Freeman
    ad Mar 29, 1856, b Jan 11, 1843, d 1915
Josephine Lawton Greene w/o Mallory - ad Mar 29, 1856, d Jul 11, 1909
Coralinn Greene White w/o Herman - d/o Orilla Jones & Lorenzo
    ad Mar 29, 1856, b Jan 27, 1832, d Jan 24, 1897
Mary Corey Trowbridge w/o Gould - ad Mar 29, 1856, d Aug 7, 1917
Dr. Zacheues R. Babcock s/o Mary Reynolds & Amos - prob fr Petersburg
    ad Jul 4, 1857, d Jun 24, 1889
Laura Maxson Babcock w/o Zacheus - ad July 4, 1857, d Nov 9, 1886

Adelaide Coon d/o Dorcas Vars & J. Greene - ad Dec 2'56, d Jun 1, 1900
Chas Coon s/o Mary Crosby & Ransom - ad May 1, 1858
    b Jan 30, 1835, d May 7, 1911
E. Curtis Crosby s/o Lucretia Greene & Samuel - ad May 1, 1858
    b Feb 19, 1835, d July 23, 1906
Quincy DeForest Greene s/o Ann Sweet & Thos H. - ad May 1, 1858
    b June 25, 1840, d Aug 28, 1831
Dea. Geo. W. Gardner s/o Almira Hunt & Geo. -ad Jul 24'58, d Nov 17, 1914
Roswell Clark s/o Martha Babcock & Nathan Jr - ad May 3, 1862
    b Nov 29, 1813, d Dec 27, 1891
Amelia Greene Clark w/o Roswell - d/o Mary Gavitt & Jos.
    ad May 3, 1862, b Aug 29, 1814, d Dec 26, 1900
Malone S. Babcock s/o Almira Burdick & Samuel - ad May 3, 1862
    b June 16, 1849, d Dec 7, 1940

p. 6
DeAlton Porter Greene s/o Eunice Lee & Jas. G. - ad May 3, 1862
    b Nov 6, 1845, d July 7, 1923
Albert R. Babcock s/o Lucy Lee & Nelson - ad May 3, 1862
    b Jan 1, 1847, d Apr 25, 1925
Silas Whitford Maxson s/o Marg't Whitford & Silas - ad May 3, 1862
    b Feb 29 1846, d June 9, 1916
Eugene Clark s/o Amelia Greene & Roswell - ad May 2, 1862
    b Jan 8, 1847, d Sep 6, 1880
Lois Maxson Langworthy w/o Russel - ad May 3, 1862, d Nov 10, 1904
Esther Langworthy Maxson w/o N. M. Lamphere, 2nd wid/o Lyman Maxson
    ad May 3, 1862, dis Jan 15, 1879
Marissa Dewey Greene w/o M. DeChois - d/o Eliza Green & Joel
    ad May 3, 1862, b June 12, 1844, d Dec 15, 1922
Flora Coon Babcock w/o Albert - d/o Dorcas Vars & John Greene Coon
    ad May 3, 1862, d Feb 7, 1922
Angenora Washburn Tremaine w/o Ansel - d/o Celia Greene & Freeman
    ad May, 1862, b Aug 4, 1847, d Jan 9, 1927
Adelaide Loomis Trowbridge w/o John Riley - d/o Phebe Loomis & William
    ad May 3, 1862, d Feb 2, 1882
Mary Ambrosia Greene Crandall w/o Ben - d/o Harriet Felt & Harrison
    ad May 3, 1862, b June 18, 1841, d Mar 11, 1926
Ann Elizabeth Greene Dealing w/o Foster M. - d/o Hannah Jones & Paul Jr
    ad May 3, 1862, b Nov 27, 1844, d Dec 2, 1919
Eliza Greene Lewis w/o Frank - d/o Hannah Jones & Paul Jr
    ad May 3, 1862, b Sep 9, 1846, d June 26, 1900
Rosetta O. Greene Coon w/o Henry - d/o Hannah Jones & Paul Jr
    ad May 3, 1862, b May 5, 1848, d Jan 14, 1906
Rosaline Greene Whitford w/o A. O. H. - d/o Laura Greene & Alva G.
    Greene; ad May 3, 1862, b July 16, 1849
Louise Washburn Greene w/o Franklin J. - d/o Sophia Kellogg & Moses
    ad May 3, 1862, b 1831, d Jan 6, 1893
Phebe Loomis Williams 2nd w/o Amos - ad May 24, 1862, d Mar 1904
Sally Greene Greene w/o Orsan D. - d/o Mary Clark & Reeves
    ad May 24, 1862, b Sep 15, 1848
Celestine Greene d/o Orilla Jones & Lorenzo - ad May 24, 1862
    b Aug 24, 1848, d May 17, 1912
Ann Bloodgood Utter w/o John - ad May 24, 1862, d June 17, 1901
Philo Greene s/o Orilla Jones & Lorenzo - ad Apr 25, 1863

b Apr 7, 1843, d June 9, 1913
Susanna Seldon Main w/o Jas. - d/o Elizabeth Moore & Jas.; grandmother
    of Dean Main - ad Nov 5, 1864, b Oct 11, 1796, d May 30, 1879
Pardon Babcock - ad Jan 5, 1865, d Dec 30, 1893
Polly Sweet Lee d/o Olive Greene & Eleazer Sweet - ad Jan 5, 1865
    b Feb 24, 1807, d June 5, 1899
Sarah Greene - ad Jan 5, 1865, b Mar 5, 1821

p. 7
Phebe Greene Phillips w/o Nelson - ad May 1865, d Apr 1, 1917
Orson C. Greene s/o Laura Greene & Alvah Greene - ad Mar 5'66, b Sep 24'59
Aldro Whitford s/o Charlotte Heath & Nathan - ad Mar 5'66, d Nov 12, 1928
P. Stillman Maxson s/o Betsey Brown & Jesse - ad Mar 5'66, d Mar 1, 1904
David S. Coats s/o Lois Maxson & Benj. - EX May 3, 1891
Jas C. Heath s/o Betsey Kellogg & Albert - ad Mar 5, 1866
    b June 2, 1845, d Nov 17, 1915
Adnah H. Greene s/o Samantha Lee & Horace - ad Mar 5, 1866
    b Jul 30, 1839, d Nov 6, 1915
Ella White Elmer w/o Theron, d/o Coralinn Green & Herman
    ad Mar 5, 1866, b Apr 6, 1873, d Mar 5, 1905
Emma Greene Goss Hodge w/o Orsemus, 2nd Jay Hodge - d/o Laura Greene &
    Alvah G. Greene; ad Mar 5, 1866, b Apr 27, 1851
Eudora Rogers Greene wid/o Jos Burdick, 2nd w/o Dan'l - d/o Eunice Lee &
    Jas. G. Greene; ad Mar 5, 1866, b May 29, 1849, d Feb 17, 1925
Harriet A. Davis w/o Lewis Briggs - ad Mar 5, 1866, EX May 3, 1891
Inez R. Maxson d/o Marg't Whitford & Silas - ad Mar 5, 1866, dis Feb 3'90
Francis Millard Greene w/o Adnah G., d/o Almira Fox & Samson
    ad May 5, 1866, d July 1, 1940
Ellen Wright d/o Delia Kellogg & George - ad Mar 5, 1866, d Aug 14, 1918
Emerette G. Wright Whitford w/o Aldro, d/o Delia Kellogg & George
    ad Mar 5, 1866, d Jan 22, 1914
Celestine Greene Maxson w/o S. Whitford, d/o Alvira Benj. & Bailey
    ad Mar 5, 1866, b Nov 2, 1846, d Dec 25, 1902
Omelia Potter Saunders w/o Ed - d/o Laura U. Greene & Samuel
    ad Mar 5, 1866, b July 7, 1844, d June 12, 1898
Eva Greene Hodge w/o Jas - youngest ch/o Hannah Jones & Paul Jr
    ad Mar 5, 1866, b Aug 11, 1855, d Dec 1, 1919
Delia Greene Trowbridge w/o William - d/o Cordelia Sweet & Franklin
    ad Mar 5, 1866, d Dec 13, 1919
Sarentha A. Coats d/o Lois Maxson & Benj. - ad Mar 24, 1866, d 1920
Medora Trowbridge Crandall w/o George - d/o Gould; ad Mar 24, 1866
    d Nov 5, 1890
Octavi Utter Heath w/o Andrew - d/o Ann Bloodgood & John
    ad Mar 24, 1866, b Apr 1, 1839, d Aug 11, 1885
Delia Kellogg Wright Green wid/o George Wright, 2nd w/o Thos. R. Green
    d/o Adah Maxson & Luke - ad May 4, 1866, d Sep 11, 1895
Sylvia Green Oatman w/o Darius - d/o Lydia Greene & Edward
    ad May 4, 1866, b Feb 18, 1814, d Apr, 1894

p. 8
Jacob Titsworth came from Plainfield - ad Aug 31, 1867, d Nov 20, 1889
Asa Spencer d/o Eunice Greene & Job - ad Mar 14, 1867, b Feb 27, 1826
Lyman Saunders s/o Miranda Reynolds & Joel - ad Mar 14'67, d Oct 14, 1920

Loretta Greene Saunders w/o Lyman - d/o Samantha Lee & Horace
    ad Mar 14, 1867, b May 8, 1841, d Dec 3, 1919
Orville Potter s/o Laura Greene & Samuel - ad Mar 21, 1867
    b Sep 19, 1847, d Apr 12, 1922
Foster M. Dealing s/o Sarah Greene & Benj. - ad Mar 21, 1867
    b Mar 10, 1842, d Nov 1, 1921
Amy Greene Babcock, w/o Malone - d/o Alvira Benjamin & Bailey
    ad Mar 21, 1867, b Oct 22, 1850, d Dec 7, 1940
Ella Spicer Conant d/o Dea. Edw Spicer - ad Mar 21, 1867, EX May 6, 1877
Martha Kellogg Cotton w/o Willis - d/o Juliet Grommon & Isaac
    ad Mar 21, 1867, EX May 5, 1879
Oscar Scrivens s/o Cath Greene & Daniel - ad Mar 28, 1867
    b July 14, 1848, dis May 8, 1898
DeEsting Utter s/o Ann Bloodgood & John - ad Mar 28, 1867
    b Feb 26, 1841, EX Nov 4, 1888
Gertrude Greene Utter w/o DeEsting - d/o Selinda Greene & Gideon Greene
    ad Mar 28, 1867, b July 20, 1847, d Feb 12, 1886
Samuel A. Bates s/o Abagail Stowell & Merrik M. - ad Mar 28, 1867
    b Nov 22, 1834, d May 1876
Henry Chase s/o Betsey Miner & Roswell - ad Mar 28, 1867, d Apr 1904
Alice Hull Langworthy w/o Caleb, - d/o Marg't Sweet & Frank
    ad Mar 28, 1867, d July 8, 1904
Florence Brundidge Thomas w/o Bayard - d/o Susan Greene & Almanson B.
    ad Mar 28, 1867, b July 1857, EX July 4, 1880
Jennie Greene d/o Mary Adelia Scrivens & Leander R. - ad Mar 28, 1867
    b July 12, 1853, d Aug 8, 1887
Jane Robbins Main w/o Orange - ad Mar 28, 1867, d Dec 5, 1902
Dan'l Chase bro/o Henry - ad Apr 4, 1868, d Apr 1882
Susan Countryman w/o Dan'l Chase - ad Apr 4, 1868, EX May 5, 1895
Albert Babcock fr Verona - ad July 4, 1868, b July 6, 1814, d May 8, 1884
Orletta S. Greene w/o Albert - d/o Susannah Williams & Caleb
    ad July 4, 1868, b Feb 11, 1815, d Mar 8, 1890
Benj F. Gibbs hus/o Jeanette Greene - ad Sep 5, 1868, d Feb 1895
Eliza Ann Wise w/o Asa Spencer - ad Sep 5, 1868, EX Jan 6, 1889

p. 9
Annette Millard Maxson w/o Christopher - d/o Almira Fox & Sampson
    ad Sep 5, 1868, d Oct 17, 1904
Pearlie Burdick Greene w/o Leonard R. - d/o Eumelia Wheeler & Albert
    ad Oct 3, 1868, b May 29, 1843, d Nov 17, 1919
Rev. A. B. Prentice - pastor 1/3 Century; s/o Eliza Babcock & Allen P.
    ad Nov 7, 1868, b July 29, 1838, d May 24, 1904
Monroe Maltby s/o Calvin - ad Mar 6,'69, b Sep 28'38, d Apr 16, 1927
Saphronia Lee Maltby w/o Monroe - ad Mar 6, 1869, d Apr 2, 1929
Naomi Greene Witter w/o Jas - d/o Betsey Kenyon & Jos
    ad May 22, 1869, d Oct 27, 1817, d July 7, 1891
Murray Maxson s/o Marg't Whitford & Silas
    ad Sep 18, 1869, dis Chicago Church

Dr. Edwin S. Maxson s/o Dr. Edwin R. - ad Sep 18 1869
    dis to Syracuse Feb 19, 1891, d 1933
Sarah Maxson Cobb w/o Herbert - d/o Lucy Lanphear & Dr. Edwin R.
    ad Sep 18, 1869; EX; d 1917
Martin Titsworth s/o Jacob - ad Apr 23, 1870, d Aug 3, 1915

William Trowbridge s/o Henrietta & Oren
    ad Apr 23, 1870, b Dec 26, 1847, d Aug 17, 1923
Edson Eugene s/o Hannah Jones & Paul Greene Jr
    ad Apr 23, 1870, b May 20, 1850, d Jan 8, 1907
Fred K. Hefflon moved to CA - ad Apr 23, 1870, EX Nov 5, 1882
Caleb Langworthy s/o Marg't Greene & Morris - ad Apr 23, 1870
    b Feb 12, 1851, d Nov 13, 1925
William Spicer s/o Eliza Wells & Dea. Ed - ad Apr 23, 1870, d 1879
Emma Hull Greene 2nd w/o DeFrance - d/o Marg't Sweet & Franklin
    ad Apr 23, 1870, b Mar 26, 1851, d Dec 10, 1911
Mary Utter Kellogg w/o Eli - d/o Ann Bloodgood & John
    ad Apr 23, 1870, d July 14, 1939
Emogene Langworthy Greene w/o Eugene - d/o Marg't Greene & Morris
    ad Apr 23'70, b Nov '28, d Nov 11, 1913
Mary Babcock Merriam w/o Morris - d/o Orletta S. Greene & Albert
    ad Apr 23, 1870, b July 20, 1852, EX Jan 6, 1889
Lydia Crandall Munderback w/o Henry - d/o Eleanor Sherman & John
    ad Apr 23, 1870, b Apr 13, 1843, d Nov 1, 1905
Ida Greene Kellogg w/o Frank - d/o Laura Green & Alvah
    ad Apr 23, 1870, b Oct 30, 1854, d Oct 31, 1919
R.R. Woodward - ad Apr 22, 1871, d Feb 3, 1901
Mary Dryden Scrivens w/o Oscar - d/o John; ad May 13, 1871, EX May 8, 1898
Abel G. Lewis s/o Abraham Lewis of Petersbirg - ad Aug 26, 1871, d Apr 2'82
Martha Babcock Lewis w/o Abel - ad Apr 26, 1871, d 1881

p. 10
Ellen Kellogg Titsworth w/o Martin - d/o Adah Maxson & Luke
    ad Aug 26, 1871, d Feb 24, 1924
Morris Langworthy s/o Nancy Babcock & Saunders
    ad Aug 26, 1871, b Oct 9, 1914, d Feb 2, 1886
Marg't Greene Langworthy w/o Morris - d/o Susannah Williams & Caleb
    ad Jan 5, 1872, b Apr 10, 1816, d Sep 14, 1904
Walter Brundidge s/o Lucy Greene & Dan'l - ad Aug 3'72, EX Jan 2'87
Martha Bell Graham 2nd w/o DeEsting Green - d/o Abagail Overton & Lyman
    Bell wid/o Graham; ad Aug 3, 1872, b Sep 5, 1831, d July 20, 1906
Elizabeth Maxson Clark w/o George R. - d/o Julia Ward & Joseph
    ad Aug 3, 1872, d May 22, 1876
Judson Clark s/o Amelia Greene & Roswell - ad Sep 5, 1872
    b Feb 9, 1852, EX Mar 5, 1905
Alma Washburn Clark w/o Judson - d/o Schuyler; ad Sep 7'72, EX Mar 5, 1905
Dea. Amos Stoodley s/o Elizabeth Lane & William; ad Oct 12, 1872
    b Apr 13, 1845, d Jan 31, 1930
Francis Clark Stoodley w/o Amos - d/o Mary Maxson & Welcome
    ad Oct 12, 1872, b Apr 27, 1874, d Oct 21, 1906
Chester Crandall s/o Fanny Frink & Delos; ad Oct 12, 1872, EX May 1882
Geo R. Clark s/o Amelia Greene & Roswell - ad Feb 8, 1872
    b Dec 31, 1849, EX Mar 5, 1905
Seraphine Sisson Clark w/o Eugene - ad Feb 8, 1872, d July 4, 1882

Horace Greene s/o Sally Saunders & John - ad Mar 7, 1874
    b Apr 4, 1807, d Apr 29 1882
Samantha Lee Greene w/o Horace - d/o Eunice & Angel Lee
    ad Mar 7, 1874, b Dec 31, 1810, d June 10, 1886

Palmer Whitford Greene s/o Polly Burdick & Saunders
    ad Mar 28, 1874, b Oct 11, 1811, d June 15, 1885
Freelove Williams Greene w/o Palmer Whitford Greene -d/o Freelove & Henry
    Williams; ad Mar 28, 1874, b Feb 6, 1803, d Aug 3, 1895
Mary A. Greene Greene w/o William M. - d/o Freelove Williams Greene &
    Palmer Whitford Greene; ad Mar 28, 1874, b Apr 6'37, d Dec 5, 1907
Nelson Wood s/o Lucinda Potter & Geo - ad Apr 4, 1874, d Dec 16, 1886
Chas Trowbridge s/o Henrietta Jones & Orrin - ad Apr 4, 1874, EX
Chas Spicer s/o Dea. Edw & Mary Stillman - ad Apr 4, 1874, EX Nov 2, 1879
Willis Brundidge s/o Susan Greene & Almanson Bridge
    ad Apr 4, 1874, b Aug 1862, living
Ada Clark Emerson w/o Gilbert - d/o Marie C. & Edwin Clark
    ad Apr 4, 1874, b Nov 5, 1856, d 1908
Addie Greene Sheldon w/o Orsan J. - d/o Francis Millard & Adnah
    ad Apr 4, 1874, b June 26, 1861, d Aug 7, 1939
Libbie Wright Langworthy w/o John - d/o Lucy Jones & Lewis
    ad Apr 4, 1874, d Sep 19, 1928
Jesse Whitford s/o Charlotte Heath & Nathan - ad May 23'74, d Mar 10, 1934

p. 11
Lizzie Babcock Maxson w/o Corridon - d/o Clarissa Benj. & Pardon
    ad May 23, 1874, dis W. Edmeston Aug 1, 1883, d June 1, 1942
Susie Evelyn Ayers Barney w/o Dr. Herbert - niece/o Mrs. C.D. Potter
    ad May 23, 1874, EX Mar 20, 1910
Maretta Stone Patterson w/o John - ad May 30, 1874, d Feb 13, 1931
Perrin Crandall s/o Fanny Frink & Delos - ad May 23, 1874, EX May 5'95
Dea. Judson A. Horton s/o Emeline Dickson & Cornelius U.
    ad May 31, 1874, b Jan 1856, living
Amelia Brundidge d/o Lucy Greene & Dan'l - ad May 31, 1874, EX May 5,1895
Hannah Gilbert Maxson w/o Benj. - ad May 31, 1874, d May 18, 1891
Lucinda Patrick d/o Bryon - lived at Dea. Harvey Barton's
    ad Nov 7, 1874, d Dec 18, 1876
Orletta S. Babcock Potter w/o Orville - d/o Sophronia Green & Albert
    ad Nov 6, 1875, b Jul 18, 1849
Ed B Saunders s/o Dea. Roswell & Sophia Pennington Saunders
    ad Jan 29, 1876, d Oct 26, 1918
Fred Saunders s/o Amelia Potter & Dea. Roswell - ad Jan 29'76, Ex May 8'98
John Patterson came fr Ireland -ad Jan 29, 1876, d. 1905
Matilda White d/o Coralinn Greene & Herman
    ad Jan 29, 1876, b Jun 4, 1863, EX
Ann M. Greene Tomlinson w/o Everett - d/o Melissa Greene & O. DeGrass
    ad Jan 29, 1876, Jan 1,1800, d 1944
Hanna M. Britton d/o Melissa Greene & O. DeGrass -ad Jan 29'76,b May 25'61
Eliza Gardner Kenyon w/o Herbert - d/o Delia Potter & Geo
    ad July 29, 1876, dis to Westerly
Hetty Wright d/o Lucy Jones & Lewis - ad July 29, 1876, d Aug 21, 1920
Sam'l Crosby s/o Lucretia Babcock & E. C. - ad July 29'76, Ex May 5'95
Lillian Davis, mother a sister of Angeline Babcock
    ad Jul 29, 1876, d Oct 24, 1883
Lucy Prentice Stillman w/o Alfred S. - d/o Marion Greene & Rev. A. B.
    ad Jul 29, 1876, b Aug 6, 1861
Lewis Wright s/o Isaac & Betsey - ad Feb 5, 1876, d Feb 7, 1901
Theron Elmer - ad Feb 5, 1876, EX

Fay D. Greene s/o Josephine Maxson & DeForest
    ad Feb 5, 1876, b Dec 14, 1861. d May 29'39
Hatty White Oyer w/o Chas - d/o Coralinn Green & Herman
    ad Feb 5, 1876, b Sep 22, 1860, EX May 5, 1895
Ella Sloddard Maxson w/o Alden - ad Feb 5, 1876, EX May 5, 1895

p. 12
John Langworthy lived with Morris Langworthy
    real name Mumpkin; ad Feb 5, 1876
Homer Greene s/o Orilla Jones & Lorenzo
    ad Feb 5, 1876, b May 12, 1838, d May 30, 1883
Albert Crandall - ad Feb 12, 1876, EX May 5, 1895
Anna Maltby Vitter 4th w/o E. A. - d/o Saphronia Lee & Monroe
    ad Feb 12, 1876, d Nov 20, 1940
Anna Greene Averill w/o Chas - d/o Josephine Lawton & Mallory
    ad Feb 12, 1876, b Mar 4, 1864, d Nov 27, 1927
Herman White s/o Oliver & Permilia White
    ad Feb 12, 1876, b Mar 27, 1830, d Mar 24, 1906
Albert G. Glass s/o Sophia Greenly & Lorenzo
    ad Feb 19, 1876, b June Mar 8, 1840, d Jan 27, 1927
Irving Babcock s/o Orletta S. Greene & Albert
    ad Feb 19, 1876, b June 3, 1857, d Sep 1904
Joseph Hull s/o Marg't Sweet & B. F. - ad Feb 19, 1876
    b Dec 20, 1862, d Mar 12, 1836
Caroline Lee Babcock w/o Chas H. - d/o Polly Sweet & Benj.
    ad Feb 19, 1876, b Nov 23, 1840, d Mar 30, 1888
Esther Jones Trowbridge w/o Orrin - d/o Betsey Randall & William
    ad Feb 19, 1876, d Oct 7, 1913
Chas H. Babcock s/o Lucinda Maxson & Russel B. - ad Feb 19'76, EX Mar 4'88
Nettie Stone - ad Mar 4, 1876
Nellie Saunders 2nd w/o D. Porter - d/o Loreta Greene & Lyman
    ad Mar 4, 1876, b June 24, 1860, d Dec 21, 1842 (1942 ?)
Arthur Greene s/o Louisa Washburn & Franklin J. G.
    ad Mar 4, 1876, b Jan 16, 1863, d July 19, 1934
Delbert F. Greene s/o Louisa Washburn & Franklin J. G.
    ad Mar 4, 1876, b Nov 28, 1860, d 1899
Philander Trowbridge s/o Esther Jones & Orrin - ad Mar 4, 1876
Mary Greene Prentice 2nd w/o A. B. - d/o Nancy Perry & Ira
    ad Jul 7, 1877, b Oct 22, 1837
Amanda Titsworth Tomlinson w/o Geo - d July 21, 1877
Lena Tomlinson d/o Amanda - ad July 21, 1877
Cora Tomlinson d/o Amanda - ad July 21, 1877
Levi Walsworth - ad Sep 29, 1877, dis Jan 2, 1898
Estelle Waterbury Walsworth w/o Levi - ad Sep 29, 1877, d Apr 15'22
William D. Ayars neph/o Mrs. Correl Potter - ad Sep 29. 1877
Welcome Clark - ad Mar 1, 1887, d Feb 20, 1902
Mary Maxson Clark w/o Welcome - d/o Dea. Holly (of Scot?)
    ad Mar 1, 1878, d July 19, 1892

p. 13
Frank Lewis s/o Martha Babcock & Abel - ad Mar 1 1878
Julia Greene Webb Folsom w/o Josiah Webb - d/o Mary Coon & G. Wash
    ad Mar 1, 1878, b July 20, 1862, d June 1938

Martha Coon Graves w/o Fred - d/o M. Satera Green & Chas
    ad Mar 1, 1878, b Nov 24, 1861, d Oct 1, 1932
Chas A. Babcock s/o Saphronia Greene & Albert - ad Mar 9, 1878,
    b Apr 12, 1846, d Dec 8, 1922
Ella Williamson Babcock w/o Chas A. - d/o Judith Slaughter & Geo
    ad Mar 9, 1878, d Oct 5, 1934
Ella Chase Wood w/o Nelson - ad Mar 9, 1878, Ex May 8, 1898
Phebe Otis Richardson - ad Mar 9, 1878, EX May 3, 1891
Mary Ladd Horton 2nd w/o A.J. - ad Mar 9, 1878, d May 29, 1917
Samuel David - ad Mar 23, 1878, EX May 5, 1895
Mrs. Samuel David - ad Mar 23, 1878, d Dec 1936
Lewis Greene s/o Frances Millard & Adnah
    ad Apr 6, 1878, b June 5, 1863, d Apr 1899
Lucy Jones Wright w/o Lewis - d/o Betsey Randall & William
    ad Apr 6, 1878, d Oct 24, 1897
Carrie Myers Bartlett w/o Fred - ad Feb 28, 1879, EX Sep 6, 1885
Rev. Alex Campbell - ad Feb 28, 1879, dis 1884
Thos. Spicer - ad Apr 10, 1880, d Jan 6, 1895
Louisa Spicer w/o Tho. - ad Apr 10, 1880, d Aug 27, 1914
Fannie Greene Saunders w/o Thos. - d/o Mary Greene & William G.
    ad Apr 10, 1880, b Sep 1, 1866, d June 5, 1910
Louise Green w/o Ewd. - d/o Betsey Brown & Jesse Maxson
    ad Jan 6, 1882, d Jan 6, 1902
Wealthy Williams Overton d/o Mary Chapman & John
    ad Feb 11, 1882, dis Sep 6 1885
William S. Maxson s/o Celestine Greene & S. Whitford
    ad Feb 18, 1882, b Apr 13, 1867, d Aug 18, 1937
William P. Jones, Dea. for 30 yrs, s/o Abagail Saunders & T. P.
    ad Feb 18, 1882, b Nov 1, 1869, d Dec 4, 1940
Frank S. Jones s/o Abagail Saunders & T. P. - ad Feb 18'82; living
Harold Tomlinson s/o Amanda Titsworth & Rev. Geo
    ad Feb 18, 1882; killed Jan 1900
Harrison White s/o Coralin Greene & Herman
    ad Feb 18, 1882, b Mar 15, 1886, EX Oct 10, 1925
Paul B. Dealing s/o Ann Elizabeth Greene & Foster
    ad Feb 18, 1882, b Sep 26, 1870
Grace Dealing Lindsey w/o Chas - d/o Ann Elizabeth Greene & Foster
    ad Feb 18, 1882, b June 9, 1933
Lucy Crosby Harring w/o Chas - d/o Lucretia Babcock & E. C.
    ad Feb 18, 1882, b May 8, 1868

p. 14
Ida B. Greene Rich w/o Elisha d/o Medora Maxson & William DeFrance
    ad Feb 18, 1882, b June 4, 1865
O. D. Greene Jr s/o Melissa Greene & O. D. - ad Feb 18'32, b July 12'68
Seth Trowbridge s/o Esther Jones & Orrin - ad Feb 18, 1882
Henrietta Trowbridge wid/o Ernest Stevens, 2nd w/o Clayton Langworthy
    ad Feb 18, 1882
Marg't Greene Place w/o Phil - d/o Josephine Maxson & Q. DeForest
    ad Feb 18, 1882, b Mar 15, 1867, dis Alfred, d Oct 8, 1938
Amy Greene d/o Josephine Maxson & Q. DeForest
    ad Feb 18, 1882, b Sep 19, 1870; living
Nettie Greene Miller w/o Ed - d/o Josephine Lawton & J. Mallory
    ad Feb 18, 1882, b Sep 23, 1866

Anna Witter Spring niece/o Naomi Greene Witter - ad Feb 18, 1882; living
Emma Main d/o Jane Robbins & Orange
    ad Feb 18, 1882, b Jul 20, 1772, d May 19, 1888
Delia Maxson Wallace w/o David - d/o Christopher Maxson
    ad Feb 18, 1882, dis Apr 5, 1913
Louisa Goss d/o Emma Greene & Oresmus - ad Feb 18, 1882, d Oct 25, 1886
Martha Lewis d/o Eliza Adelaide Greene & Frank
    ad Feb 18,1882, b Sep 15, 1872, dis
Susan Williams Gurley w/o David - Mary Chapman & John
    ad Feb 18, 1882, b June 18, 1865, d Oct 12, 1945
Rose Glass Ayars w/o William - d/o Alzina Crosby & A. G.
    ad Feb 18, 1882, d June 21, 1894
Mary Whitford Williams w/o Jesse - d/o Rose Greene & A. O. H.
    ad Feb 18, 1882, b May 2, 1869, dis to Verona
Norris Lee Maltby s/o Sophronia Lee & Monroe - ad Feb 28'82, dis Jan 4'25
Mary S. Maxson - ad Feb 25, 1882; (can't trace)
Mary J. Greene Owens w/o Milton - d/o Mary J. Coon & G. Wash.
    ad Feb 25, 1882, b Aug 25, 1867, d Aug, 1943
Pearlie Whitford Strictland w/o William - d/o Emerette Wright & Aldro
    ad Feb 25, 1882, dis; living
Ella Greene Thomas w/o Clark, wid/o Lewis Greene - d/o Ann Coon &
    D. Porter Greene; ad Feb 25, 1882, b Sep 25, 1865, d Aug 18, 1944
David S. Gurley s/o Augusta Greene & Harrison D.
    ad Mar 11, 1882, b Jan 24, 1867, d Sep 23, 1937
Geo. Tomlinson s/o Amanda Titsworth & Rev. Geo. - ad Mar 11, 1882, dis
Benj. Maxson Greene adopted s/o Mary Hull & Andrew J.
    ad Mar 11,1882, d Apr 1946
Geo. S. Bates eldest s/o Cindarilla Greene & Samuel A.
    ad Mar 11, 1882, b Sep 20, 1869, d Sep 11, 1884
Sheldon S. Bates s/o Cindarilla Greene & Samuel A.
    ad Mar 11, 1882, b Apr 22, 1869, dis 1898; living
p. 15
Martha B. Langworthy d/o Annie Lanphere & Daniel - ad Apr 1, 1892; dis
Tressa M. Greene d/o Louise Maxson & Ed ad Apr 1, 1892
Fred Greene s/o Louise Maxson & Ed - ad Apr 1, 1892, dis Nov 4, 1888
Diantha Maxson d/o Dea. Holly - ad July 15, 1892, d Jan 20, 1891
Jay Hodge s/o Charlotte Munson & Rodney
    ad July 22, 1892, b Jan 8, 1854, EX May 5, 1895
Grant Davis s/o Emma Dickinson & Samuel
    ad July 22, 1892, dis to Milton Apr 27, 1929;
Viola Davis Williams 2nd w/o Jay - d/o Emma Dickinson & Samuel
    ad July 22, 1892; living
Mrs. Caleb Bailey - ad July 29, 1892, d June 28, 1900
Foster D. Clark - s/o Amelia Greene & Roswell
    ad May 12, 1893, b Mar 4, 1863, EX Mar 5, 1905
William D. Scrivens s/o Lemira Coon & Zebulon J.
    ad July 12, 1893, b June 1, 1869, d June 16, 1942
Manford D. Greene s/o Marissa Dewey & DeChois
    ad May 12, 1893, Ex Mar 5, 1905, d Nov 11, 1938
Nellie Dealing Picket w/o John - d/o Sarah Greene & Benj.
    ad May 12, 1893, d Mar 17, 1893
Dora Chase Trowbridge w/o Frank - d/o Ursula Maxson & Henry
    ad May 12, 1893; living
Mary Holloway Saunders - ad 15, 1894, EX Jan 7, 1923

Flora Wright Chapin - ad May 17, 1894
Gilbert Emerson - ad May 24, 1894, EX Mar 5, 1905
Myron S. Brundidge s/o Susan Greene & Almanson B.
    ad May 24, 1894, b Feb 11, 1865, d 1944
Eliza Prentice w/o Allen - mother of Rev. A. B.
    ad Sep 6, 1894, d Apr 30, 1892
John Williams s/o Marg't Saunders & Jos. - ad Mar 8'85, d Apr 9, 1915
Albert Greene s/o Mary Clark & Reeves
    ad Apr 25, 1885, b Nov 26, 1865, d Oct 10, 1922
Clifford H. Coon s/o Rosetta O. Greene & Henry
    ad Apr 25, 1885, b July 2, 1872; dis Mar 1902 to NY; living
Dr. Francis L. Greene s/o Pearlie Burdick & Leonard R. G.
    ad Apr 25, 1885, b Aug 18, 1869; living
Clara Kenyon Crosby w/o Samuel - d/o Delia Beals & Ed
    ad Aug 25, 1885, EX May 5, 1905
Ida Cady Hull w/o Joseph - d/o Chas, ad Apr 25, 1885, d Aug 12, 1933
Mahala Glass sister of A. G. - ad Apr 25, 1885, d Oct 12, 1901

p. 16
Ruth Bannister d/o Lewis - ad Apr 25, 1885, EX May 5, 1905
Jesse U. Greene Coon w/o Clifford H. - Josephine Maxson & Q. DeForest
    ad Apr 25, 1885, b Aug 2, 1872, dis to NY, d 1942
Harriette Witter Greene w/o Fay - d/o Fanny Clark & Delos
    ad Apr 25, 1885, b Mar 29, 1869, dis Leonardsville Jan 31, 1891
Marg't (Minnie) Trowbridge Whitford w/o Ed - d/o Esther Jones & Orrin
    ad May 25, 1885, living
Mary Ordway Maxson w/o Murray - d/o Ira (?)
    ad May 9, 1885, dis to Chicago
Fred A. Graves hus/o Martha Coon - ad May 9, 1885, d May 7, 1888
Chas Lindsey s/o Carrie Daly & Henry - ad May 9, 1885, d Mar 25, 1934
Nelson Phillips - ad May 9, 1885, d Mar 1921
Kate Johnson Sisson w/o Arthur - niece/Welcome Clark
    ad May 9, 1885, dis Sep 24, 1892
Etta Wright Greene w/o Bert - d/o Lois Greene & Pliny, living
Emma Trowbridge d/o John Riley - ad May 9, 1885, EX May 8, 1898
Darius Potter s/o Mary J. Greene & Bailey - ad May 9'85, May 8, 1898
Della Babcock w/o Willis - d/o Mary J. Greene & Bailey
    ad May 9, 1885, d July 17, 1945
Jay Williams s/o John & Welthea - ad May 9, 1885, dis to Milton
Emily Peckham Williams 1st w/o Jay - ad May 9'85, Ex Mar 5, 1905
Jesse Williams s/o Mary Chapman & John
    ad June 6, 1885, dis to Verona, d Oct 17, 1938
Ella Davis (can't trace) - ad June 6, 1885, EX May 8, 1898
Harry W. Prentice s/o Marion Greene & Rev. Asa B.
    ad June 6, 1885, b Oct 26, 1873, dis to NY
S. Maria Stillman Williams w/o Thomas R. - teacher A.C. School
    ad Nov 7, 1885, dis Jan 9, 1889
Sarah Greene Dealing w/o B. D. - d/o Abagail G. & Martin
    ad Nov 7, 1885, d Oct 1894
Clarissa Pool - (can't trace) ad Mar 6, 1886
Caleb Bailey - ad June 5, 1886; dis by letter
Mrs. W. J. Colton (Martha Kellogg) d/o Juliet Grommons & Issac
    ad Dec 31, 1886, b Sep 22, 1822, d Nov 10, 1907

Ida Greene Kellogg w/o Frank - d/o Laura U. Greene & Alvah Greene
    ad Mar 4, 1887, b Apr 30, 1854, d Oct 31, 1919

p. 17

Myra Saunders Scrivens w/o William D. - d/o Loretta Greene & Lyman
    ad May, 1887, b Oct 19, 1972; killed by accident June 25, 1939
Alfred C. Prentice s/o Marion Greene & Rev. Asa B.
    ad May 21, 1887, b Feb 18, 1875; living
Mrs. Thompson W. Saunders - ad Oct 1, 1887 (letter); d Oct 25, 1884
Salinda Greene Greene w/o Gideon - d/o Mercy Sheldon & Rev. William
    ad Oct 1, 1887, b May 23, 1811, d Sep 24, 1902
Whitford P. Greene s/o Mary Greene & William M.
    ad Jan 21, 1888, b Dec 3, 1874, EX May 8, 1898; living
Frank Lester (can't trace) ad Jan 21, 1888, EX May 1898
Curtis Scrivens s/o Mary Dryden & Oscar
    ad Jan 21, 1888, b Jul 17, 1873, EX May 1898; dead
Jesse Brundidge s/o Susan Greene & Almanson
    ad Jan 21, 1888, b July 17, 1873, EX May 1898
Edwd Whitford s/o Rose Greene & A. O. H.
    ad Jan 21, 1888, b Apr 4, 1873, d Sep 26, 1945
Samuel Fox Bates youngest ch/o Cindarilla Green & Samuel A.
    ad Jan 21, 1888, b Feb 17, 1875, June 3, 1946
Clark Stoodley s/o Francis Clark & Dea. Amos - ad Jan 21, 1888; living
Dea. Chester Williams s/o Mary Chapman & John - ad Jan 21'88; living
Arlie Hurd Barrett w/o Chas - gr-niece/o Mrs. Spicer Greene
    ad Jan 21, 1888, d May 1, 1903
Bertha Whitford Oatman w/o William - d/o Rose Greene & A. O. H.
    ad Jan 21, 1888, b Nov 8, 1874
Jennet Clark 2nd w/o Ed - d/o Betsey & William Jones
    ad Feb 18, 1888, d June 27, 1907
Mercy Greene Langworthy 1st w/o Clayton - eldest ch/o Emagene Langworthy &
    Eugene; ad Feb 18' 88, b Nov 25'74, d Jun 16'30
Eunice Greene Maxson w/o Orange - d/o Ann E. Coon & D. Porter
    ad Feb 18, 1888, b Jul 27, 1871; living
Teresa U. Greene Greene 2nd w/o Andrew J. - d/o Lydia G. & Alonzo
    ad Mar 6, 1888, b Apr 24, 1836, d Apr 26, 1928
Dr. Frank Clark s/o Seraphina Sisson & Eugene -ad Mar 19'88, Ex Mar'05
Chester David s/o Samuel - ad Mar 19, 1888, EX May 1895
Holly Maxson s/o Celestine Greene & S. Whitford
    ad Mar 19, 1888, b Nov 20, 1874, d Sep 15, 1927
Eva Trowbridge Eastman 2nd w/o Herbert - d/o Dea. Gould
    ad Mar 19, 1888, d May 1, 1931
Frances Greene d/o Selenda & Gideon Greene
    ad Mar 19, 1888, b Apr 8, 1850, d July 28, 1890
Mattie Gibbs Wilson w/o George - d/o Henry & Martha Horton; adopted by
    Jeanette Green & Benj. Gibbs; ad Mar'88, d Apr 6, 1934
Mary David Keller w/o O. L. d/o Samuel Davis - ad Mar 19'88, EX May'95

p. 18

Lenche Lee Deacon w/o Sylvester - d/o Polly Greene & Benj.
    ad May 19, 1888, d June 23, 1901
Charlotte Kenyon w/o Justin who was brother of Betsey Kenyon Greene
    ad by letter July 7, 1888
Josiah Webb hus/o Julia Greene - ad Dec 14, 1889, d Dec 20, 1889

Belle Greene Greene w/o Arthur - d/o Laura Brooks & Palmer
    ad Jan 2, 1890, b Sep 20, 1862, d July 24, 1925
Lucy Hart Davis 2nd w/o Samuel - ad June 7, 1890, d Mar 17, 1907
Hattie Taylor Heath 2nd w/o Andrew - ad June 7, 1890, d Mar 10, 1914
Lepha Greene Hovey Babcock w/o Fred - d/o Ann E. Coon & De A. Porter
    Greene; ad June 7, 1890, b Aug 5, 1873
Alice Williams Sisson w/o Bert - d/o Mary Chapman & John
    ad June 7, 1890, EX Apr 1916
Minnie Lyman niece/o Fred Graves - ad June 28, 1890, d Jan 24, 1891
Oren Durham - ad May 2, 1991, d 1920
Mrs. Oren Durham - ad May 2, 1991, d Dec 22, 1913
Enoch Colton - ad May 9, 1891, d Feb 10, 1909
Ardellia Holley Greene w/o O. D. Jr - ad Aug 8'91, dis Jan'10; living
E. Curtis Crosby s/o Lucretia Greene & Samuel
    ad Jan 16, 1892, b Feb 19, 1838, d July 22, 1906
Matilda Greene Whitford Gurley 2nd w/o Harrison, wid/o Jay Whitford;
    d/o Margy Drake & Wells K. - lived with Elder Quible
    ad Jan 16, 1892, b Jul 23, 1836, d Jan 22, 1924
Henry C. Glass s/o Alzinia Crosby & A. G. - ad Apr 23'92, d Feb 13, 1913
Orange Maxson s/o Christopher - ad Apr 23, 1892, EX Mar 5, 1905
Lora Maxson s/o Christopher - ad Apr 23, 1892, EX Apr 5, 1913
Frank Langworthy s/o Alice Hull & Caleb - ad Apr 23, 1892; living
Ernest DeChois Greene s/o Emagene Langworthy & Eugene
    ad Apr 23, 1892, b Apr 6, 1879; living
Chas Chase s/o Ursula Maxson & Henry - ad Apr 23'92, EX Mar 5'05, d '41
Jay Greene s/o Dan'l - ad Apr 23, 1892, EX Mar 5, 1905
Roy D. Greene s/o Medora Maxson & DeFrance
    ad Apr 23, 1892, b Jun 2, 1879, d Feb 28, 1942
Jay Greene s/o Ann E. Coon & D. Porter
    ad Apr 23, 1892, b Aug 3, 1876, dis Mar 5, 1905
Bailey Greene s/o Dan'l - ad Apr 23, 1892, dis Mar 5, 1905

p. 19
Francis Williams s/o Leland K. - ad Apr 23'92, EX Jan 8'22; living
Bess P. Greene Lord w/o Morris - d/o Pearlie Burdick & Leonard R.
    ad Apr 23, 1892, b Dec 29, 1875, d Mar 24, 1899
Mary Crosby Vitter 3rd w/o E. A. - d/o Juliette Hull & Henry
    ad Apr 23, 1892, b May 16, 1873, d June 17, 1935
Rena Glass Bunce d/o Alzina Crosby & A. G. - ad Apr 23'92, Ex Mar 5, 1905
Marian Greene d/o Josephine Maxson & DeForest
    ad Apr 23, 1892, b June 11, 1879, d Aug 9, 1919
Kate Bunce - ad Apr 23, 1892, d Nov 14, 1901
Flora Spicer Carley w/o Francis - adopted by Thomas Spicer
    ad Apr 23, 1892, d Mar 12, 1902
Alice Greene Reed 2nd w/o Geo - d/o Dan'l, ad Apr 23, 1892, dis July'39
Eugene R. Coon s/o M. Satira Greene & Chas
    ad May 7, 1892, b Sep 2, 1870, Ex Mar 5, 1905, d Jan 24, 1910
George Whitford s/o Emmerette Wright & Aldro - ad May 7, 1892; living
Horace Saunders s/o loretta Greene & Lyman
    ad May 7, 1892, b July 8, 1874, Ex May 8, 1898, living
Frank G. Chase s/o Ursula Maxson & Henry - ad May 7'92, EX Mar 5, 1905
Cartha Clark Brown w/o Lori - d/o Seraphine Sisson & Eugene
    ad May 7, 1892, EX May 8, 1898

Mary Babcock Jones 1st w/o Frank - d/o Ella Williamson & Chas
    ad May 7, 1892, d Apr 23, 1930
Nettie Potter Woodward w/o Jasper - d/o Laura U. Greene & Samuel M.
    ad May 7, 1892, b Dec 8, 1869, d July 27, 1942
Jane Greene Worder w/o Micajah - adopted d/o Mary Hull & Andrew J.
    ad May 7, 1892, Ex Mar 5, 1905
Bessie Kellogg Glass w/o Henry - d/o Ida Greene & Frank
    ad May 7, 1892, b Dec 10, 1877; living
Jesse Barney Greene w/o Frank - niece/o Mrs. S. W. Maxson
    ad May 7, 1892, Ex Mar 5, 1905
Marg't Williams d/o Leland K. - ad July 16, 1892, d Nov 23, 1936
Dora Babcock d/o Caroline Lee & Chas H. - ad July 16, 1892, Ex Mar 5'05
Samuel A. Davis s/o Eunice Hinman & Samuel -ad Jan 16'93, d Mar 20'03
Leland K. Williams s/o Marg't Saunders & Jos.
    ad Aug 27, 1893, d Apr 23, 1918
Mrs. Leland K. Williams - ad May 27, 1893, d Mar 13, 1910
Arlouine Williams d/o Nancy King & Jos. - ad Apr 21'94, d Jan 15, 1943
May Greene d/o Mary Pitcher & Edwin - ad Apr 21, 1894, Ex Mar 5, 1905
Jennie Greene d/o Mary Pitcher & Edwin - ad Apr 21, 1894, EX Mar 5, 1905

p. 20
Sara Louise Greene d/o Pearlie Burdick & Leonard R.
    ad Apr 21, 1894, b Nov 4, 1881, d Jan 19, 1902
Mrs. Mable Greene Thomas d/o Francis Millard & Adnah - w/o Thomas
    ad Apr 21, 1894, b Aug 4, 1878, EX Mar 5, 1905
Eva Austin Bates w/o S.F. - d/o Emma O. Wait & Dempster C.
    ad Apr 21, 1894, b Jan 8, 1877; living
Bertha Williams d/o Nancy King & Jos. - ad Apr 21, 1894; living
Marion Barrett Fry w/o Thomas - d/o Eliza Cagwin & Henry
    ad Apr 21, 1894, b Dec 19, 1880, EX 1924
Sadie Reed Clark w/o Foster - ad Apr 28, 1894, EX Mar 5, 1905
Fred Thomas s/o DeWitt - ad Apr 28, 1894, EX May 8, 1898
Frank Trowbridge s/o Esther Jones & Orrin - ad May 18'95, d Jan 23'99
Marg't Greene Stoodley w/o Clark - d/o Emagene Langworthy &
    E. Eugene; ad May 18, 1895, b Aug 3, 1883; living
Clayton Langworthy - ad by letter Mar 1896, d June 16, 1896
Janie Whitford Cornwall Bakker w/o Garrelt Bakker - d/o Hattie Kellogg &
    Jesse; ad Mar 1896; living
Clara Hull Greene w/o Roy D. - d/o Ida Cady & Jos. - ad Mar 1896
Dr. Arthur C. Graves s/o Martha Coon & Fred - ad Mar 1896, Ex Jan 8'22
Mary F. Graves w/o Sherman Keegan - d/o Martha Coon & Fred
    ad Mar 1896, dis Jan 1, 1921
William F. Oatman - ad 1898; living
Dora Williams w/o Grant - ad 1900; living
Laura Trowbridge Baggs d/o Dora Chase & Frank -ad May 19, 1900, dis Jul'39
Hanna Horton Greene w/o DeChois -d/o Mary Ladd & A. J.; ad May 1900
Anna Williams d/o Emily Peckham & Jay - ad May 19, 1900
    dis Oct 20, 1904; living
Elizabeth Krake Stratton 1st w/o Sheldon - lived with Caleb Langworthy; ad May 19, 1900, dis Oct 20, 1904; living
Frederick Langworthy s/o Alice Hull & Caleb
    ad May 19, 1900, d July 27, 1912
Rev. Sylvester Powel, pastor - ad May 17, 1902, dis 1915
Sarah E. Powell w/o Slyvester - ad May 17, 1902, dis 1915

Miriam G. Powell d/o Slyvester - ad May 17, 1902, dis 1915
Olive M. Powell d/o Slyvester - ad May 17, 1902, dis 1915
Paul R. Powell s/o Slyvester - ad May 17, 1902, dis 1915
Helen Powell d/o Slyvester - ad May 17, 1902, dis 1915

p. 21
Frank Griswold - ad May 17, 1902, EX Jan 27, 1923
Mrs. O. D. Cornwall - ad July 30, 1904, d Feb 13, 1926
Helen Whitford Hoke w/o Clarence, d/o Dora Chase & Frank Trowbridge
    adopted by Ed & Minnie Whitford - ad July 30, 1904
Harold Whitford - see above
Blanche Webb Finley d/o Julia Greene & Josiah - ad July 30, 1904
Ruby Greene Nichols w/o Jerry, d/o Etta Wright & Bert
    ad July 30, 1904, d Oct 26, 1918
Paul Greene s/o Emagine Langworthy & Eugene - ad July 30, 1904,
    b Feb 6, 1889, living
Anna Gurley d/o Susan Williams & David S. - ad July 30, 1904
    b Oct 12, 1891, d May 13, 1913
Nellie Dunham Kerch d/o Owen - ad Sep 10, 1904, EX
Eva Greene White w/o Ernest, d/o Belle Greene & Arthur Greene
    ad Sep 10, 1904, dis to NY Dec 1936,
Mahala Greene Cook Greene wid/o Jason Cook, 2nd w/o O.D. Greene
    d/o Margy & Wells K. Greene - ad Oct 22, 1904, b Feb 6, 1844
    d Jan 26, 1928
Gilbert Horton s/o Mary Ladd & Dea. A.J. - ad May 9, 1903; living
Kenneth F. Horton s/o Mary Ladd & Dea. A.J. - ad May 9, 1903; living
Allie Dealing Lewis w/o Welcome, d/o Elizabeth Kellar & Martin
    ad June 2, 1904
Adelaide Jones d/o Nettie Trowbridge & Delos - ad July 30'04, Ex Nov 4'16
Rev. E. H. Socwell, pastor - ad July 1, 1905, dis Jan 16, 1909
    d Jan. 30, 1930 at Nady AK
Mrs. E. H. Socwell - ad July 1, 1905, dis Jan 16, 1909
Lillian Socwell d/o E. H. & LIllian - see above
Chas Socwell s/o E. H. & Lillian - ad Aug 4, 1906, dis Jan 16,1909
Almira Sheldon Greene Brewster wid/o William Greene w/o R. C.
    d/o Addie Greene & Oscar - ad July 1, 1905, b May 26, 1888
Clara Belle Williams Crosby w/o Clifford d/o Mary Whitford & Jesse
    ad July 1 1905
Maude Greene d/o Etta Wright & Bert - ad July 1, 1905
Carl Greene s/o Belle Greene & Arthur Greene -ad Jul 1, 1905
    dis Aug 3, 1946
Blanche Langworthy w/o Frank - ad Sep 9, 1905, living
Matie Lawton Williams w/o C. C. - ad Sep 9, 1905
    b Apr 29 (year not given) d Aug 16., 1939
Mary Hull Reed w/o Elwyn d/o Ida Cady & Jos. - ad Sep 9, 1905
    b. Aug 1, 1888, dis Oct 8, 1827

p. 22
Harold Langworthy s/o Mercy Greene & Clayton - ad Aug 4, 1906, living
Eva Gurley Jones 2nd w/o Frank d/o Susan Williams & David S.
    ad Aug 4, 1906, b Dec 19, 1884, living
Alda White Butterfield d/o Herman White - ad Aug 4, 1906
    dis Mar 20, 1910, living

Anna Scrivens d/o Myra Saunders & William - ad Aug 4, 1906
    b Jul 22, 1894, d Oct 27, 1945
Rev. E. A. Vitter, pastor - ad Jan 2, 1909, dis Jan 2, 1914
Almeda Vitter w/o E. A. - see above
Eva Vitter Horton w/o Kenneth d/o E. A. - see above

Ann G. Washburn Tremaine w/o Ansel d/o Celia Greene & Freeman
    ad May 1, 1909, b Aug 4, 1947, d Jan 9, 1927
Ernest Williams s/o Dora & Grant - ad Jan 1, 1910
Grace Vitter Ladd w/o Harry d/o E. A. - ad Jan 1, 1910, living
Chrlottr Crumb Davis w/o Grant - ad Jan 1, 1910, dis Apr 27, 1929
Inez Maxson d/o Marg't Whitford & Silas - ad Jan 2'11, d Mar 25'18
Lottie Miner Fredericks w/o Delbert F. - ad May 6, 1911
Francis Carley s/o Flora Spicer & Francis - ad May 6'11, dis Oct 10'25
Carl Williams s/o Dora & Grant - ad May 6, 1911, living
Ralph Greene s/o Belle & Arthur - ad May 6, 1911, living
Reata Langworthy Ruud w/o Willard d/o Libbie Wright & John
    ad May 27, 1911, living
Hazel Langworthy Brock d/o Libbie Wright & John
    ad May 27, 1911, living
Gordon Langworthy s/o Libbie Wright & John - ad May 27, 1911
    b Sep 27, 1898, d Oct 17, 1935
Virgil Langworthy s/o Libbie Wright & John - ad May 27'11, living
Mrs. Samuel David - ad May 27, 1911, d Dec 1936
Clara Saunders Maltby w/o Norris - ad Sep 1, 1900, d Jul 20, 1923
Ernest Stevens - ad Mar 7, 1914, d Nov 8, 1929
Gladys Scrivens Chrysler w/o Herbert d/o Myra Saunders & William
    ad Mar 7, 1914, b Aug 10, 1899, living
Delberta Vitter Greene w/o Gerald d/o Rev. E.A. - ad Mar 7'14, living
Isobel Vitter Hamilton w/o Jas. d/o Rev. E.A. - ad Mar 7'14,dis Apr 1'14
Ellen Williams Houghlaling w/o Paul d/o Mary Whitford & Jesse
    ad Mar 7, 1914, living

p. 23
Rev. A. Clyde Ehret, pastor - ad Feb 13, 1913, dis Oct 1, 1920
Clella Ford Ehret w/o Clyde d/o Laura Davis & Samuel - see above
Ella Heath Whitford w/o Harold - ad Feb 13, 1915
Calvin Maltby s/o Clara Saunders & Norris L. - ad Mar 20'15, dis Jul'39
Lawrence R. Maltby s/o Clara Saunders & Norris L.
    ad Mar 20, 1915, d Mar 11, 1931
Bernice Maltby Davis w/o David d/o Clara Saunders & Norris L.
    ad Mar 20, 1915, dis to Shiloh Jul 27, 1935
Rev. Leon M. Maltby s/o Clara Saunders & Norris L. - ad Mar 20, 1915
    dis Apr 20, 1932
Bertha Fassett - ad Mar 20, 1915, dis Jul 1939
Laura Greene Vithington Frink w/o Leslie wid/o William Vithington
    killed WW I, d/o Belle & Arthur Greene - ad Mar 20'15, living
Irene Sisson d/o Alice Williams and Bert - ad Mar 20, 1915
    dis Apr 20, 1916
Ethel Williams Rice d/o Mary Whitford & Jesse - ad Mar 20, 1915
    dis to Verona May 1920 (entry crossed out for some reason)

John Williams s/o Mary Whitford & Jesse - ad Mar 20, 1915
    dis to Verona May 1920

Earl Williams s/o Mary Whitford & Jesse - ad Mar 20'15, dis May'16
Minnie Williams d/o Dora & Grant - ad Mar 20, 1915,
Mrs. Harriuson White - ad Mar 20, 1915, d Feb 13, 1928
Madeline White Raglan d/o Mrs. Harrison White - ad Mar 20'15, dis Jul'30
Frances Lindsey d/o Grrace Dealing & Chas. -ad Mar 20'15, dis Feb 2'19
Orrin Stevens s/o Henrietta Trowbridge & Ernest -ad Mar 20'15, d Mar 21'18
Sadie King Whitford w/o Geo. d/o Clara Leonard & Alonzo
    ad May 1, 1913, living
Hattie Kellogg Whitford w/o Jesse d/o Mary Jane Fuller & Geo.
    ad (no date given), d June 7, 1918
Rev. Loyal F. Hurley, pastor - ad Aug 31'21, dis Sep 8'33
Mae Van Horn Hurley w/o Loyal - see above
Mildred Saunders Greene w/o Paul - ad Sep 24, 1921, living
Evelyn Glass Keuchle w/o Manuel d/o Bess Kellogg & Henry C.
    ad Sep 24, 1921, b Aug 1904
Evelyn D. Greene Avery w/o DeWilt d/o Hanna Horton & DeChois
    ad Sep 24, 1921, b Aug 12, 1907
Gerald H. Greene s/o Hanna Horton & DeChois - ad Sep 24'21, b Nov 1'05

p. 24
Kent Stoodly s/o Marg't Greene & Clark - ad Sep 24, 1921
Mildred Parker Maltby Scrivens wid/o Lawrence Maltby, w/o Harold
    d/o Jennie Brownell & Newton - ad Sep 27, 1921
Wilson Maltby s/o Clara Saunders & Norris - ad Sep 24, 1921
Nellie Mae Parker Barbur d/o Jennie Brownell & Newton - ad May 27, 1922
Lyle P. Langworthy s/o Libbie Wright & John L.
    ad May 27, 1922; killed in Germany Jan 21, 1945
Alice Langworthy Blackman w/o H. V. - d/o Blanche & Frank
    ad May 27, 1922; living
Foster D. Lindsey s/o Grace Dealing & Chas - ad May 27, 1922; living
Marion I. Greene d/o Maude Greene - ad May 27, 1922; living
George W. Greene s/o Belle & Arthur - ad May 27, 1922; living
Harold Scrivens s/o Myra Saunders & William -ad May 27'22, b Oct 10'03
Cornelius Verry s/o Wouternyte Putman & Cornelius
    ad June 17, 1922, b Holland
Alida Verry d/o Marie Remmers & Matthias Von Dommelin
    ad June 17, 1922, b Holland
Samuel Dibble - ad May 26, 1923
Lora Greene w/o Samuel - d/o Venell Saunders & D. Porter -ad May 26'23
Delberta Vitter Greene w/o Gerald H. - d/o Rev. E.A., ad May 16'25
Clark Saunders bro/o Mrs. Norris Maltby - ad Nov 7, 1925
Clara Saunders w/o Clark - ad Nov 7, 1925
Edith Saunders w/o Gould d/o Clark - ad Nov 7, 1925
    dis to Alfred Apr 12, 1941
Earl Saunders s/o Clark - ad Nov 7, 1925
Joyce E. Greene d/o Mildred Saunders & Paul - ad Nov Nov 21, 1925
Doris E. Greene Heath w/o Webster d/o Mildred Saunders & Paul
    ad Nov 21, 1925
Wilfred S. Greene s/o Mildred Saunders & Paul - ad Nov 21, 1925
Mary Verry Bird w/o George - d/o Cornelius, ad Nov 21, 1925
Ross C. Stoodly s/o Marg't Greene & Clark - ad Nov 21, 1925
Nathan Whitford s/o Sadie King & George - ad Nov 21, 1925
Nellie Verrey d/o Cornelius - ad Nov 4, 1927
Mrs. Harold Scrivens d/o Jay Greene - ad Nov 4, 1927

Jay Maltby s/o Clara Saunders & Norris - ad Nov 4, 1927

p. 25
Sherman Trowbridge s/o Delia Greene & William - ad Sep 3'27, b Apr 18'74
Louise Webster Trowbridge w/o Sherman - d/o Lucy Dodge & John Wesley
    ad Sep 3, 1927, b Sep 16, 1874
Dr. Wesley W. Trowbridge s/o Louise Webster & Sherman
    ad Sep 3, 1927, b Nov 26, 1894
Alice Peckham - ad Oct 8, 1927, d June 4, 1932
Christopher Langworthy s/o Edwina Clark & Fred'k - ad May 26, 1928
Frances Waters Langworthy w/o Christopher - ad May 26, 1928
Fred Babcock - ad May 26, 1928, d Mar 7, 1932
Edna Webster sis/o Mrs. Sherman Trowbridge - ad May 26, 1928
Garrelt F. Bakker s/o Afren Smit & Free'k J. - ad Nov 24, 1928
Nellie Smith Trowbridge w/o Wesley W. - ad Nov 26, 1928
John Sherman Trowbridge s/o Mary Denny & Wesley
    ad Nov 26, 1928, b Sep 22, 1918
Emogene Greene d/o Mildred Saunders & Paul - ad Nov 26, 1928
Holly Whitford s/o Ella Heath & Harold - ad Nov 26, 1928
Meriam Hurley Charles w/o Russell - d/o Rev. L. F. - ad Nov 26, 1928
Helen Austin Curtis niece/o Mrs. S.F. Bates
    ad Nov 26, 1928, b Mar 31, 1920, dis Nov 22, 1941
Barbara Horton Gilmore w/o Albert - d/o Bertha Palms & Gilbert
    ad Aug 30, 1928,
Walter F. Newton s/o Lorinda Hosmer & Orrin -ad Dec 6'28, d Jan 1'33
Miza Pettengill Newton 2nd w/o Walter - d/o Caroline Sayle & Eastman
    ad Feb 21, 1931, d Jan 10, 1932
Bertha Palmer Horton w/o Gilbert - ad Jul 25, 1931
Mrs. Flora Sleter - ad June 24, 1933, dis Jul July 5, 1936
Dr. Louis R. Conradi - ad Oct 22, 1932
    b Karlsruhe, Germany Mar 20, 1826, dis Dec 19, 1932
Mary Ellen Greene Reed w/o Chauncey - d/o Hanna Horton & DeChois
    ad June 24, 1933, b June 10 (birth incomplete)
Marjolyn Horton Gilmore w/o Allen - d/o Bertha Palms & Gilbert
    ad June 24, 1933
Mary Belle Wilson Adams w/o John H. - Mattie Gibbs & ??, ad Jun 24'33
Mary Emma Stillman Williams w/o Orville - gr.dau/o Rev. E.A. Witter
    ad June 24, 1933, dis to Verona Feb. 8, 1944
Francis Greene s/o Mildred Saunders & Paul - ad June 24, 1933

p. 26
Juanita Hurley Garcia w/o Ed - d/o Rev. L.F., ad Jun 24'33, dis Sep 18'33
Rev. Orville W. Babcock, pastor - ad Sep 1934
Mabel Butts Babcock w/o Orville - ad Jun 17'38, dis Salemville Oct'33
Welcome H. Bakker s/o Garrelt Bakker - ad June 17, 1938
Ruth Dibble d/o Lora Greene & Samuel - ad June 17, 1938
LaVerne Maltby s/o Mildred Parker & Lawrence - ad June 17, 1938
Alfrieda Maltby d/o Mildred Parker & Lawrence - ad June 17, 1938
Ruth Clement Maltby d/o Jay Maltby - ad June 17, 1938
Ronald Greene s/o Mildred Saunders & Paul - ad June 17, 1938
Rev. Paul S. Burdick, pastor - ad Nov 8, 1941, dis June 18, 1945
Hansey Burdick w/o Paul - see above
Stanley Burdick s/o Paul - see above
Victor Burdick s/o Paul - see above

Marion Burdick d/o Paul - see above
Esther Burdick d/o Paul - ad Jul 18, 1942, dis June 18, 1945
Emma Burdick d/o Paul - see above
Robert Burdick s/o Paul - see above
Lois Horton d/o Bertha Palms & Gilbert - ad Aug 10, 1040
Judson Horton Greene s/o Delberta Vitter & Gerald H.
    ad Aug 10, 1940, b June 10, 1927
Gareth Greene s/o Delberta Vitter & Gerald H. - ad Jul 5'44, b Apr 30'29
Arden Greene s/o Delberta Vitter - ad Jul 5'45, b Jun 6' 34
Priscilla Ladd gr.d/o Rev. E. A. Witter - ad Aug 1940
LeRoy Burdick s/o Rev. Paul - ad July 5, 1944
Fred'k Langworthy s/o Frances Waters & Christopher - ad Jul 5'44
Beatrice Maltby d/o Mildred Parker & Lawrence - ad Jul 5'44
David Avery s/o Dorothy Evelyn Greene & DeWitt
    ad Apr 19, 1945, b Oct 16, 1933

        MS 1947.1 CRR   vault
      Arranged And Compiled 1945-6
          by Mrs. S. F. Bates

IMS: 1993

HOUNDSFIELD 1841-1872
Jefferson Co. NY

Subscribers

George Frink	Nancy Frink
Elias Frink	Almyra Frink
Israel F. Burdick dis	Alzina Frink
Daniel B. Burdick	Marilla Brown
Perry W. Burdick	Diantha Maxson
Silas Maxson f/o S. W. of Alfred	Temperence Burdick
Nelson Clarke	Maria Crandall
Henry Brown	Sarah M. Clarke May'63
Reuben W. Utter	Mary E. Utter dis
Charles West	Esther West
Steven Clarke d 1841	Judith Clarke
Holly W. Maxson	Lucy W. Maxson
John Utter Jr	Annie E. Utter
Asa M. Green	Ruth Brown d 1847
Daniel J. Brundidge d 1880, 74 yrs	Lucy Brundidge
Lorenzo E. Mattison d 1848	Betsey Fuller
Roswell Clarke	Nancy Witter
Dea. Benjamin Maxson from Adams d 1874	Judith Wood
Samuel C. Bassett	Aurelia L. Burdick
Joel Green	Nancy Green rj Oct 15'68
William Green	Mercy Green
John T. Witter	Lencha Greene
William C. Crandall	Elvira Greene
Willard L. Converse	Phebe Converse
Wesley Gardner	Olove Gardner rj
Patience Witter	Amelia Clarke
Lodema Clarke	Sarah Witter
Julia Maxson	Hannah Coon dis
Sally Ann Maxson	Electa Truman
Perrin Frink	Leater Greene
Nathan R. Truman f/o Alvin of Alfred	David Coon Jr
Joseph C. Maxson	Nelson Woodward

Rev. Enoch Barnes s/o Sally Barnes - ad May 28, 1848
b Nov 28, 1791, Jun 9, 1877

Woolsey Spicer	Roxanna Spicer
Christian p. Green	Hannah Green
Welles H. Green ad Jan 13'69	Roxanna Green
Almanson Brundidge ad Feb 4'69	Oliver Brundidge
Lieuren Bennett	Charles E. Green
Welcome Clarke	Mary Clarke
Delos Crandall	Deborah L. Bennett
Fanny Frink Crandall w/o Delos	Adelaide E. Utter ad May 19'69

Oramel Frink Barton w/o Dea. H. C. - May 19'69
Emily Crandall Frink Cobb ad May 19'69
Hannah T. Maxson w/o B. J.

Additional Names after 1849

Charlotte Phillips	Prudence Witter
George P. Burdick	Waity Burdick
Victoria Utter	Octavi Utter

Sarah Larribee
Freelove Green
Palmer H. Green

The Record of the Seventh Day Baptist Church of Houndsfield,
Jefferson Co. NY
June 3, 1841-Oct 27, 1872
CRR 19x.56   vault   IMS:1993

WATSON (Lowville)
1841- 1908 Lewis Co.

Charter Members
from Adams

Dea. Joseph Stillman   Lucy Stillman
Esther Stillman   Amos R. W. Stillman
Harriet Stillman   Clark Burdick
Polly Burdick   Marian Clark
David Barber   Jane R. Barber
William G. Quible   Eliza Ann Quible
Wells K. Green
Woolsey Spicer   Roxanny Spicer
Daniel S. Andrews   Almeda Andrews
Joseph Green   Elizabeth Green
Caroline Barber   Joshua Clark

from 1st Brookfield

Sophia Burdick   Roxannah Green
Calvin Clark   Nancy Clark
Ezra Whitford   Polly Whitford
Joseph A. Nye

from 2nd Brookfield

Elisher (sic) Davis   Luetta Davis

from 1st Verona

George Davis   Fanny Davis
Anna Davis   Sarah Larabee
Benjamin Davis Jr   Canace Jane Davis
Amanda Swan   Joseph B. Davis
Bathsheba M. Davis   G. Dervina Davis
Susan Davis   Sarah Allen
Parmer W. Green   Jacob Burdick
Daniel P. Williams   Lucind Williams
John Munpford   Barbary Munpford
Sarah Munpford   Amy Susan Mumpford

from 2nd Verona

Stephen R. Burdick	Elizabeth Burdick
Eunis Burdick	Mary Burdick
Zackeus Burdick	Nancy Peckham

from Petersburg
Benjamin Burdick

from Otselic
John E. Rodes   Susannah Rodes

from Truxton
Edwin Church   Eunice Church

History of the Seventh Day Baptist Church of Watson
sketch by B. F. Stillman, clerk
He states he worked from poor records.
Church Records B File   IMS:1993

RICHLAND
Jefferson Co. NY 1845-c.1855

Members

Obediah Johnson - b 1766 Middletown, CT; bp at 16, moved to Richlands
 & converted to Seventh Day Baptist beliefs in 1816
 d Jan 27, 1846

Rev. Elias Burdick, pastor - d Mar 20'70, 72 yrs	Mrs. Burdick
Dea. V. V. Hubbard - clerk, d 1859	Mrs. Hubbard
Leonard Seman	Walter Menter
Mrs. Menter	Mercy Payne d 1850
Brayton Slater	Mrs. Slater

The Notebook of C. H. Greene
B file   IMS:1993

DIANA
Lewis Co. 1846-
(also called Pitcairn, St. Lawrence Co.)
16 members
no primary records extant

S.S. Coon, pastor   G. P. Burdick, deacon
R. S. Greer, clerk

SDB Year Book 1946   IMS:1993

PINCKNEY
(also called Sandy Creek)
Lewis Co. NY 1848-c.1910
no primary records extant
20 members

William J. Somes, pastor   C. Green, clerk
    SDB Memorial Vol I, p. 95   IMS:1993

CENTRAL NY STATE INDEX

ACHLEY, 32 62
ADAMS, 17 111
ALEXANDER, 45
ALLEN, 29 32 40 41 48 65 67 68 73 84 88 114
ALLIS, 15
ALMON, 81
AMES, 38 44
AMEYDEN, 86 91
ANDREWS, 114
ANGEL, 11 12
ANNAS, 41 46
ANNIS, 16
ANTHONY, 16 48
ARMSTRONG, 38
AUSTIN, 24 61
AVERILL, 101
AVERY, 110 112
AYARS, 7 9 10 15 31 101 103
AYERS, 48
AYRES, 11
BABCOCK, 2-6 8-11 14 15 17-20 23 26 28 30-32 34 36-38 40 42 46-49 61-67 71 78 80 82 86 92 94 96-98 101 102 104 106 107
BACHUS, 49 64 82
BAGGS, 107
BAILEY, 2 18 19 31 32 103 104
BAKER, 9 30 49 76
BAKKER, 107 111
BALDWIN, 90
BANESTER, 76
BANISTER, 78
BANNISTER, 104
BARBER, 42 50 51 71 110 114
BARKER, 22
BARNES, 18 113
BARNEY, 100
BARRETT, 105
BARTLETT, 102
BARTON, 75 113
BASS, 8 11 14 15 17
BASSETT, 2-4 6-8 10-12 16 17 21 73 113
BATES, 98 103 105 107
BATSON, 82 90
BEAVER, 86
BECK, 89
BEEBE, 27 28
BELDEN, 16
BENJAMIN, 40
BENNETT, 22 77-81 83 85 113

BENTLEY, 18-35
BEST, 46
BETSON, 83 85
BEULL, 25
BIRD, 87 110
BISBY.2
BLACKMAN, 110
BLAKEMAN, 41
BLY, 90
BOARDMAN, 83
BORTLE, 89
BOWEN, 8
BOWMAN, 40 46
BRADT, 8
BRAND, 12 14 16-18 23
  36
BRANNON, 91
BREED, 29
BREWSTER, 108
BRINKLEY, 18
BRITTON, 100
BROCK, 109
BRODERICH, 90
BRODNICK, 40
BRODRICK, 41
BRONSON, 47
BROWN, 4-9 11-17 19
  20 22-24 33 42 44
  46 70 107 113
BROWNE, 12
BROWNELL, 13 17
BRUCE, 18
BRUNDAGE, 99
BRUNDEDGE, 94
BRUNDIDGE, 100 104
  105 113
BRYNER, 87
BUNCE, 106
BURCH, 4 9 11 12 15-
  17 20 23 25 33
BURCHEK, 41

BURDICK, 1-9 10-12
  15-42 44-47 51 52
  61-70 76-80 82 83
  88 89 91 111-115
BURNS, 31
BURTON, 16
BUSH, 90
BUTTERFIELD, 109
BUTTON, 9 10
BUTTS, 31
BYRNES, 87
CAGWIN, 78
CAMPBELL, 30 39 62 68
  81 88 89 102
CARD, 8 47 74
CARDNER, 29 32-34 43
  68-70
CARDSON, 28
CARLEY, 106 109
CARNES, 33
CARPENTER, 31 61 62
CARR, 86
CARTWRIGHT, 29 61 63
  66
CARY, 40
CASE, 40
CASTLES, 41
CHAMPLIN, 3 8 9 14 17
  21 24 29 61 87
CHAPIN, 5 20 78 104
CHARLES, 111
CHASE, 95 98 106
CHESTER, 79 80
CHURCH, 16 20 28-31
  47 64 68 73 115
CLAPSON, 17
CLARK, 18 31 32 34 36
  38 52 53 71 80-83
  94 96 99 101 103
  105 107 114
CLARKE, 1-9 10-21 23

CLARKE (Continued)
  24 28 33 36 44 113
CLAYTON, 90
CLEVELAND, 4 8
COAKLEY, 73
COATS, 6 97
COBB, 53 99 113
COCKRAN, 31
COGWIN, 80
COIL, 76
COLE, 2 3 5
COLEGROVE, 1-4 7 28-
  30 32 36 39 68 69
COLEMAN, 28
COLTON, 105 106
COMVERSE, 113
CONANT, 98
CONGDON, 7
CONGER, 76 79 82
CONRADI, 111
COOLEY, 68
COON, 1 3-6 8-10 12
  15 19-24 27-42 44-
  47 53 61-70 93-96
  104 106 113 115
CORBET, 11 24
CORNWALL, 64 108
CORWIN, 76
CORY, 28
COSSUM, 39
COTES, 2
COTTON, 98
COTTREL, 8
COTTRELL, 28 38 41 42
  53 54 64
COUNTRYMAN, 98
COVEY, 4 6 7 10 11
COWELS, 78
COY, 28 29
CRAFT, 42 44 46

CRANDALL, 1-8 10-12
  14-26 28-36 38-41
  43-46 61-69 76-78
  89 95-97 99 100
  101 113
CRAWFORD, 9
CROFS, 39
CROP, 37
CROSBY, 92 94-96 100
  104 106 108
CROSS, 39-41 90
CROWFOOT, 26
CRUMB, 1 2 6 8 9 10-
  12 14 15 20 28 30
  32-34 36-41 43 45
  46 61-63 65 66 73
CRUZAN, 91
CULVER, 70
CURTIS, 36 46 69 71
  80 111
CUTLER, 24
DANFORD, 18
DAVID, 84 102 105 109
DAVIS, 1 2 4-10 12
  14-18 25 26 30 36-
  39 62-68 71 75-87
  89 90 97 100 103
  104 106 109 114
DEALING, 96 98 102
  104
DECKER, 83 85 87
DEELY, 87
DEFEE, 47
DENISON, 10 18 19 21
DENNISON, 12
DERMOTT, 73
DEWEY, 92
DIBBLE, 110 111
DILLMAN, 84-87
DOOLITTLE, 19

DORAN, 42
DORMAN, 76 78
DORRVORD, 43
DOUGLAS, 95
DOWNER, 32
DOWSE, 7 12 14 16 31
DRACHE, 32
DRESSER, 21 23 24 26
DUNN, 33
DURHAM, 106
DUSKEE, 89
DWIGHT, 4 47
DYE, 1 5 12 29 34 37
   39 61-64 66 73
DYER, 101
EADES, 79
EASTMAN, 105
EDWARDS, 10 11 17 20
   80
EHRET, 109
ELDRAS, 31
ELLIS, 35 39
ELLISON, 16
ELMER, 97 101
ELMORE, 69
EMERSON, 100 104
EVANS, 33
FARBUSH, 21
FARGO, 86
FASSETT, 109
FAY, 89
FELTON, 23 24 89
FERGUSON, 82
FIFIELD, 73
FILEY, 86
FINCH, 67
FINLEY, 108
FISH, 47
FISHER, 35 36 65
FITCH, 17
FOLSOM, 102

FOOTE, 19
FORD, 92
FORGAR, 90
FOSTER, 19
FOX, 28 35 68
FRANKLIN, 1 2 18 83
   85
FREDERICHS, 109
FREEMMAN, 30
FRINK, 18 42 44 54 55
   109 113
FRISBIE, 42 44 55
FRISBY, 47
FRY, 107
FULLER, 113
GARCIA, 111
GARDINER, 46
GARDNER, 69 76 79 80
   93 94 96 113
GARNER, 70
GASNER, 43
GATES, 23 47
GETMAN, 86
GIBBS, 93 98
GILETTE, 33
GILMORE, 111
GLASS, 95 101 104 106
   107
GLINES, 12
GOODRICH, 12
GOODWIN, 33
GORTON, 9 18 19
GOSS, 103
GRAHAM, 17 99
GRAVES, 102 104 107
GRAY, 76
GREEN, 2 4 8 12 13 29
   34 36 55 70 75-81
   84-86 89 92 94 95
   97 102 113-116
GREENE, 6 9 19 27 28

GREENE (Continued) 40 75 92-99 100-113
GREENMAN, 1-4 6-9 28
GREENOUGH, 8
GREFFING, 71
GRIFFIN, 34
GRIFFITH, 80
GRISWOLD, 6 20 108
GROUSTELL, 76
GURLEY, 94 103 106 108
HADDEN, 76
HAKES, 36
HALL, 3 5 12 55 62
HAMILTON, 28 68 109
HARDER, 11
HARDIN, 14 16
HARRING, 102
HARRIS, 76 78 79
HARRY, 25
HART, 73
HARVEY, 64 66
HASKAL, 55
HASSARD, 75 76
HAVEN, 15
HAY, 89
HAYES, 44 55
HAYS, 38 91
HAZARD, 55 79
HAZZARD, 76
HEATH, 95 97 106 110
HEFFLON, 99
HENDEE, 66 67
HENRY, 41 44
HERRIG, 81 82 85
HESS, 89
HIBBARD, 11 12 18 19
HIGGINS, 73
HILL, 8 15

HILLMAN, 87
HILLS, 7 19
HILSON, 76
HINKLEY, 19
HINSHAW, 45
HODGE, 97 103
HOKE, 108
HOLCOMB, 30 33 35 79 81 82
HOLMES, 12 18 25 39
HOLT, 10 21 79
HOLTON, 4
HOOK, 73
HOOPER, 71
HORTON, 100 102 108 109 111 112
HOSIE, 25
HOUGHLALING, 109
HOUSE, 7 34
HOWARD, 73
HUBBARD, 56 115
HULL, 21 24 56 92 101 104
HUMPHREY, 22 73
HUNT, 56 84 85 88 89
HUNTING, 35
HUNTINGTON, 2 56
HUNTLEY, 15
HURLEY, 45 86 110
HUTCHINSON, 73
HYDE, 83-86
INGHAM, 41 64
IRAMEN, 29
IRISH, 28 29 32 34 35 43 45 68-70
ISALLY, 35
JAMES, 69
JENNINGS, 17
JENSON, 90
JERSEL, 79

JOEL, 76
JOHNSON, 2 3 27 35 38 40 62 64-67 70 115
JONES, 3 34 41 46 47 56 64 82 84 85 94 102 107 108
JUNE, 41
JUSTICE, 37 62 63 65
JUSTIS, 15 66 67
KELLER, 83 85 105
KELLOGG, 4 18 94 99 105
KELLY, 56
KEMP, 41
KENNY, 5
KENYON, 2 3 6 7 28 43 45 46 76 78 100 106
KERCH, 108
KERPP, 63
KEUCHLE, 110
KING, 6 17 88
KINGMAN, 90
KINGSLEY, 74
KINNEY, 15 39 44
KINYON, 56
KLOLYBACK, 47
KLOTZBACH, 46
KNAPP, 35 56
KNIGHT, 56
LASURE, 46
LADD, 109 112
LAMB, 16
LANGWORTHY, 1-8 12 14 18 32 34-37 63 64 78 79 84 85 96 98-101 103 105-112
LANPHERE, 4 8 9 12 15 28 71
LARKIN, 78
LARRABEE, 26
LARRIBEE, 114
LAWRENCE, 24 77-79 81 89
LAWTON, 9 11 39 76 78 79 81
LESURE, 29
LEA, 78 80 81
LEAR, 76 79
LEE, 6 9 15 97 105
LEINS, 30
LENNEN, 87
LENNIN, 85
LENNON, 83 84 86
LEONARD, 81
LERIBBINS, 77 78
LESTER, 71 105
LEWIS, 2 4 7 8-11 18 19 28 56 71 76-84 89 96 99 101 103 108
LIDELL, 42 44
LINDSEY, 102 104 110
LOCKE, 40
LOOFBOROUGH, 7
LORD, 106
LOWE, 83 85
LUTES, 76
LYING, 86
LYMAN, 106
LYON, 62
MAIN, 61 97 98 103
MAINE, 29 34 38 62 64
MALTBY, 86 98 103 110-112
MARBLE, 36 37 39 40 42 61 66 67
MARIOTT, 2 3
MARQUANT, 86
MARSH, 56 77 79-81
MARSHALL, 40 65 67
MARTIN, 5

MASON, 8 9 17
MATTISON, 8 113
MAXSON, 1-9 10-12 14
    16 17 20-36 38 40
    42 44 57 61 68 69
    71 75 77 80 90 92
    93 95-99 100-106
    109 113
MAY, 82
MCGREW, 22
MCINTYRE, 26
MCKEY, 30
MEEKER, 16
MENTER, 115
MERRIAM, 99
MIGHT, 28 33
MILLARD, 3 7 8 10 11
    22 93
MILLER, 32 86 103
MILLS, 4 5 33 47 83-
    85 88 89
MINER, 10 16
MONROE, 26 89 90
MOON, 8 9 12 71
MOONE, 69
MOOR, 7
MOORE, 11 12 83
MORGAN, 76
MULES, 41 42
MUMFORD, 77 79 114
MUMPTON, 81
MUNCY, 28 33-35 62
    64-66 68-70
MUNDERBACK, 99
MUNSON, 34
MURPHY, 12 16 18
NASH, 76
NEARY, 40
NEWCOMB, 45
NEWEY, 82 85 86
NEWTON, 35 89 111

NICHOLS, 22 24 25 28
    29 33 38 41 61-66
    108
NORRIS, 74
NORTH, 16 34 35
NORTON, 33
NOURSE, 74
NYE, 2 8 20 61 114
OAKS, 76 78
OATMAN, 97 105 107
ODELL, 45
OLIN, 28 29 61-66
ORDWAY, 23 33
OSBORN, 86
OUSLER, 43 45 46
OVERTON, 102
OVIAT, 28
OWENS, 103
PALMER, 18 19 40 41
    44 57 63-66
PALMITER, 8 9 18 22
    57 81 82 84
PALMS, 89
PARDEE, 21 82 83
PARKER, 42 44 45 47
    64
PARKHURST, 38
PARMILEE, 88 89
PARSLOW, 37 39 41 90
PATRICK, 100
PATTERSON, 100
PAYNE, 115
PEABODY, 34
PEASLEY, 33
PECK, 7 34
PECKHAM, 76 80 111
    115
PEET, 23
PERKINS, 3 5 6 16 18
    83
PERRY, 22 76-86 90

PHILIPS, 41
PHILLIPS, 9 14 15 29
    34 38 39 42 44 45
    47 68-71 74 97 104
    113
PICKET, 103
PICKETT, 42
PIDGE, 58
PLACE, 38 102
PLATT, 58
PLATTS, 8 11 33
POLAN, 26
POOL, 104
POOLE, 42 43 46
POPPLE, 4 5 9
PORTER, 11
POTTER, 1 2 10 20 22
    29 58 71 89 92 93
    95 98 100 104
POWEL, 78 108
POWERS, 74
PRAY, 58
PRENTICE, 84 98 101
    104 105
PRICE, 74
PULFORD, 30
PYE, 29 68
QUIBLE, 94 114
QUIGLEY, 33
RAGLAN, 110
RAINY, 14
RANDALL, 2 19
RAY, 25
RAYMOND, 80
REED, 23 42 106 108
    111
REES, 58
REMINGTON, 41 47
REYNOLDS, 2 10 88 89
RHODES, 83 85
RICE, 109
RICH, 102
RICHARDSON, 58 102
RICHMOND, 28-30 68
RINGE, 40
ROBERTSON, 5
ROBINSON, 9 11
RODES, 115
ROE, 90
ROGERS, 10 12 14-17
    33 34 37 38 44 58
    65-67 69 71 74
ROLLES, 40
ROLLINS, 24
ROSEN, 33
ROUNDS, 83
ROYAL, 14
RUUD, 109
SAINTJOHN, 6 11 12 15
    16 59
SANDERS, 29
SARABEE, 23
SATTERLEE, 1 45 76 81
    88 89
SATTUCK, 10
SAUNDERS, 1-5 8-11 18
    27 61 62 76 92 93
    97 98 100-102 104-
    106 110
SAXTON, 5 7 8
SCOTT, 8 58
SCRIVENS, 31 68 93 98
    99 103 105 109-111
SEALE, 26
SEALS, 58
SEAMAN, 40
SEAMANS, 7
SEAMONS, 68 90
SEARLE, 16
SELEY, 36
SEMAN, 115
SENT, 36

SHATTUCK, 79
SHELDON, 3 28 68 100
SHEPPERD, 35
SHEPPEY, 35
SHERMAN, 11 74 76 78-
 80
SHIVELY, 89
SHOLTZ, 84-87
SHOWDY, 81 84
SILK, 10
SIMONDS, 4 28
SIMONS, 5 11 14
SIMPSON, 84
SINDALL, 25 83
SISSON, 4 7-9 12 15-
 17 104 106 109
SKAGGS, 47
SLATOR, 115
SLETER, 111
SMITH, 4 8 40 41 45
 46 58 65 67 82 84
 85 87 89 90
SOCWELL, 108
SOMES, 116
SOPHER, 87
SORENSON, 87
SOULE, 74
SPAID, 90
SPAULDING, 7 9 14 17
 35
SPENCER, 2 4 5 12 18
 35 98
SPICER, 14 33 94 99
 100 102 113 114
SPRAGUE, 23
SPRING, 103
STANTON, 58
STARK, 80 82 84 85 89
STARKEY, 82
STARR, 31
STEARNS, 35

STEBBINS, 80
STEINER, 44
STEPHENS, 25 26
STEVENS, 10 109
STEWART, 11 31 40
STILLMAN, 1-11 14 15
 17-36 38-40 42 44
 46 59 61-68 74 81
 83 88 90 100 114
STILSON, 79 82 84
STIRLING, 39 40
STOKER, 46
STOLLMAN, 6
STONE, 25 37 39 62
 83-85 87 89 101
STOODLY, 99 105 107
 110
STRATTON, 107
STRICTLAND, 103
STROWBRIDGE, 81
STUKEY, 86
SUMMERBELL, 12
SWAN, 12 114
SWEENEY, 42
SWEET, 7 59
SWINNEY, 40 41
TANNER, 3 6 7
TARBELL, 11 14
TAYLOR, 2 4 85
TEIDELL, 39
THAYER, 82-85 87
THOMAS, 98 103 107
THOMPSON, 73
THORNGATE, 83-85 87
TIFT, 6
TILY, 90
TITSWORTH, 32 33 98
 99
TOLBOK, 24
TOMLINSON, 35 100-103
TRACY, 59 86 87

TREMAINE, 96 109
TRIPP, 36
TROWBRIDGE, 92 95-97
   99-102 104 107 111
TRUMAN, 45 47 59 71
   74 113
TULL, 76 78
TUTTLE, 70
TYLER, 59
UTTER, 2-4 6 9 11 13
   14 16 97 98 113
VANAIRE, 59
VANDEE, 23
VANDRESEN, 86
VANEVER, 59
VANHORN, 47 86
VERRY, 110 111
VIEROW, 85 87
VORGHT, 68
WAKEFIELD, 93
WALKER, 9 89
WALLACE, 103
WALLER, 82
WALSWORTH, 101
WALTERS, 11 15
WAMSLY, 1
WANNEN, 69
WARD, 8
WARDER, 107
WARMIS, 79
WARNER, 82-87
WARTE, 68
WASHBURN, 11 15 92 95
WATERBURY, 47
WAY, 40
WEAVER, 2 10 11 14 15
   41
WEBB, 83 106
WEBSTER, 111
WELCH, 23 26 59
WELLS, 1-3 5 17 18

WELLS (Continued)
   27-34 36-38 40 41
   44 59 61 62 68 69
WELMATH, 71
WELPEN, 34
WEST, 7-9 14 33 40 76
   86-89 113
WHEELER, 16
WHIPPLE, 91
WHITE, 3 4 7 22 24-26
   42 59 83 89 90 92
   96 100-102 108 110
WHITFORD, 1-4 6 9-12
   14-18 34 36 75 81
   93 95-97 100 104-
   106 108-111 114
WHITING, 59
WHITMORE, 10-12
WIGDEN, 1
WILBUR, 5 20
WILCOX, 2 6 7 10 23
   32-35 37 38 41 46
   59 60 64-67 79
WILLIAMS, 4 5 24-26
   30 33 42 46 71 75-
   87 89 96 103-111
   114
WILLIAMSON, 14
WILLS, 67
WILMOT, 90
WILSON, 60 105
WINCHESTER, 60
WING, 39 42 44-47
WISE, 98
WITTER, 1-5 7 8 14 20
   79-81 89 98 101
   106 109 113
WOLFE, 88 89
WONTER, 76
WOOD, 93 95 100 102
   113

WOODCOCK, 82 85
WOODWARD, 9 93 99 107 113
WOODWORTH, 80 81
WOOLWORTH, 60
WORDEN, 12 16 17
WORDSWORTH, 78
WORTH, 33
WRIGHT, 36 67 68 97 100-102
YEOMANS, 71
YORK, 40 44
YORTORS, 19

www.ingramcontent.com/pod-product-compliance
Lightning Source LLC
Chambersburg PA
CBHW062131160426
43191CB00013B/2266